SO YOU WANT TO BE AN EXECUTIVE!

SO YOU WANT TO
BE AN EXECUTIVE!

Elton T. Reeves

American Management Association, Inc.

International standard book number: 0–8144–5246–9
Library of Congress catalog card number: 73–138569

First printing

To
George, Vernon, Esther,
Darrell, Virginia, and Betty

Foreword

SOME middle managers are strongly motivated by an ambition to rise higher in the management hierarchy. In order to withstand the keen competition for executive positions, such managers must take on a truly formidable job of self-development. This book outlines the major areas of growth necessary for promotion to the executive level, and indicates some methods for achieving that growth. In the main, however, the book offers a conceptual and philosophical view of the subject rather than a how-to-do-it approach.

Elton T. Reeves

Contents

	Introduction	1
1	Why Not Stay at Base Camp?	15
2	Do You Know What It's Like at the Top?	35
3	Is Your Base Camp Secure?	56
4	What Makes You Think You're Different?	75
5	Do You Like Being the Target for Today?	93
6	How Good Is Your Crystal Ball?	114
7	What Is Your Anxiety Level Now?	135
8	Are You a Betting Man?	155
9	What's Your Game Plan?	174
10	Can You Stay There If You Get There?	195
11	What Does an Executive Owe to Society?	215
	Index	231

Introduction

YOUR desire to become an executive may have been active ever since you became a supervisor, or it may have developed within the past year or two, after you became thoroughly comfortable in a middle management job. At any rate, we can assume that you wouldn't be reading this book unless your purpose now is to become an executive.

To put things into perspective, perhaps we should look back to examine the pathway by which you got where you are now. You probably entered the management field in one of the two most common ways. Like many men, you may have come up through the ranks, after having been spotted by management as a likely candidate. Or, as is true for growing numbers of men today, you may have been recruited from your college class as a management trainee, given special treatment and planned training, and then introduced directly into the managerial stream at the beginning level.

One thing is fairly certain: Someone—either you or your superiors—gave careful thought to designing and implementing a development plan for you. Few enterprises any longer trust to luck or a kind of natural evolution to fill their managerial replacement needs. To do so would be too much like playing Russian roulette with the future of the company. Almost daily the complexity of the manager's job increases, especially in the field of decision making. The problem is no longer one of obtaining enough facts to make decisions; rather, he must be able to select the most significant data and to determine which should take priority in reaching rational and probably correct solutions to all business problems. To be successful as a middle manager, you probably had to become expert in operations research and at least somewhat familiar with the workings of electronic data processing. Neither of these systems was a necessity ten years ago; today, both are, and their importance will continue to increase in the future.

Your personnel problems are without a doubt more complex and troublesome than they were when you entered supervision. The employees now joining your organization are better educated and more sophisticated than those who were hired even a few years ago. Their personal motivations and expectations are quite different, and they are much more prone to ask penetrating questions and to demand satisfactory answers from you. Furthermore, since our civilization is a technological one, you are finding it necessary to hire many more technical, scientific, and engineering people, and these people pose some special problems to managers because of the colleague syndrome. They disregard the formalities of business organization, since their real commitment is to a profession rather than to any one enterprise. Unless you can provide them with some special answers, they will be gone like feathers on the breeze. These factors do not combine to make the manager's job any easier these days, and this trend will undoubtedly continue.

Your own case is of course different from any other person's. Your entry into supervision, your progress, your success, your advancement into middle management have been unique. But there are some problems all managers face, and development plans, although individually tailored, have many characteristics in common.

Every manager has inherent strengths and weaknesses which he must recognize and either make use of or work hard to remove. By now, you are an old pro at monitoring your development program and taking on activities aimed at accelerating your growth into a more mature and complete person. Your own professional pride will not allow you to do anything less. We can, then, make an educated guess that your progress to your present position has been the result of three major factors: natural talent, a planned system of personal growth, and some years of grueling hard work.

Since you *do* find much satisfaction in your job as a manager, the rewards are sufficient to overbalance the irritants, and your work is in the main pleasant and invigorating. But now you are again the victim of that divine discontent which we call ambition. You are wondering what you must do to get a chance at the last hurdle in the hierarchy which would put you into the executive ranks. There is this one last challenge facing you, and you will never be completely satisfied with your career until you have tested and proved yourself in this special arena.

As you prepare yourself for an executive position, you will repeat many of the activities you undertook on your way up to middle management, but you will now perform some of them with an intensity you have never experienced before. Both the tempo and the pressures will be escalated quite severely, and you must be prepared for this and be ready to accept it. The margin for error will be much smaller, and the penalties for errors will be astronomically greater.

When you have set yourself mentally and emotionally for this ordeal, take a look at what you have done as a template for what lies ahead, and start to do your serious planning. This new venture will have many of the earmarks of a complicated campaign on the battlefield: Both tactics and strategy are extremely important.

How Strong a Leader Are You?

One of your concerns in aspiring to the executive's chair is the strength of your leadership. Today's complex society demands a knowledgeable man at the head of the workforce because we interact not only among ourselves, but also with many other individuals and groups. Your decisions will be dependent upon inputs from many areas, and you will have to make value judgments which take into consideration many variables.

Your leadership strength is not quantifiable directly,

but if you will take the time and put your mind to it, both you and others can get a good idea of where you stand on a continuum of leadership ability. If you are one of the fortunate few naturally blessed with charisma, you have a definite edge over your competitors. If not, you must look to some of the commonly practiced leadership methods and techniques to carry you through. Have you developed your capacity for rapport both with individuals and with groups? Do you understand well how your people react to a given situation? Can you predict their behavior both individually and collectively? Do you have an easy time in selling your subordinates on a necessary change? Do they turn to you naturally with their work problems, or seek counsel elsewhere? Is there mutual trust and confidence both within your work group and between you and the group?

Some of these questions are of course intensely personal, and it may be embarrassing to you at first to take a hard look at the answers. Nevertheless, you must. Your leadership ability is one of the top considerations to be evaluated when those in charge consider you for advancement to the executive echelon.

It is apparent that one significant measure of your leadership will be the comparative position of your group and others in the organization. Since you undoubtedly have a diversity of functions or disciplines under your control, your group can be effective only if your presence at the helm is felt as a positive force. No other factor except your actions as a leader can truly weld your people into a group. This is another way of reiterating the old saw that a manager is made or broken by his people, rather than by his own actions directly. Your own business life has been removed from the action ever since you became a supervisor, and will continue to be so until you retire. That's the way of the business world.

At your level and at the one you hope to reach, one of the most important elements of leadership is your ability to predict your people's reactions. If you have enough empathy and understanding of them to do this well, you can make your decisions much more rapidly than can a peer who does not have this ability in the same degree. And speed of decision is of tremendous importance to you at this juncture. Later, as an executive, you will want to slow down the tempo, since your decisions will be of a long-range nature.

Getting to know your people is an exercise in sensitivity. Your immediate subordinates are also managers with their own areas of strength, their own ambitions, their own favored methods of operation. You have of course been aware of these in a general sense for some time; now you must make a special effort to synthesize all these bits and pieces into an ability to predict how they will react to specific stimuli.

The strong leader is never afraid of confrontation. In fact, on many occasions he deliberately provokes a head-on clash to settle a problem definitively. The trick is to do so with a minimum of personalities entering the picture. The battle must be intellectual and logical, with the good of the enterprise the acknowledged goal of both parties. The leader also learns to live with compromise, but he must have a fine-tuned intuition to know when compromise is not the right technique to use.

Middle management has traditionally been known as the burial ground of innovation, because the middle manager has a vested interest in maintaining the status quo.

If you are to emerge as a strong leader, you must wage constant warfare against this mental state. Certainly you must never fall into the trap of espousing change for the sake of change, but neither can you afford to lie back and dare someone to prove to you that a certain change will be for the better. It is far more to your advantage to make the necessary analyses and then judge for yourself whether a proposal has merit. The pioneer who sees correctly the value of a new tool always reaps some unique benefits.

Not that this act of innovation will in any sense be a solo effort. You will want to seek and listen to the advice of many people before making a decision on something new. There will be those whose opinions you respect; rely on them as you always have in your decision making. But the point is that *you* will make the final decision. This is your responsibility as a manager, and you can never ignore it with impunity.

At this point in your career, most of the evaluations you get of your leadership ability from others are indirect and nonverbal. Possibly your supervisor will refer to his evaluation of you in your formal performance appraisals, but for the most part you will have to take your readings of how others regard you in a more indirect way. Even so, one cue is always definitive: the frequency with which others seek your advice on matters pertaining to the job and to their job decisions. In fact, if you are a really good leader, you probably find these requests for advice a significant drain on your discretionary time; nevertheless, you know that the time you spend in this way is an integral part of your position as a manager. You are like a doctor, who cannot refuse his patients' calls upon his expertise and abilities.

What Haven't You Learned About Your Job?

Every man who works has one comforting thought going for him: No person ever does a completely perfect job. However, the man who gets the promotion is the one who remains aware of his weaknesses and does something about them on a continuing basis. You could benefit from taking a critical look at all facets of your job performance and making some judgments about the soft spots you discover.

You could start on the general assumption that a man is centered either on things or on people. For example, engineers and other technical people tend to concentrate on things. Their powers of analysis and problem solving are highly developed, but they may tend to be insensitive to nuances in interpersonal relationships. In contrast, the manager who works primarily in labor relations or employee relations will probably be oriented much less toward the mundane and inanimate parts of the job and more toward the problems of people.

This polarization has recently been recognized as the cause of major difficulties in the supervision of technical and scientific personnel. Ideally, the good manager will be aware of both orientations and will try to give his attention to both. He cannot afford to neglect either side of the coin.

Using this as a point of departure, you can analyze your performance in the four general functions of management: planning, organizing, directing, and controlling. The planning function is largely an intellectual exercise that requires your best conceptual skills, since it is concerned primarily with the establishment of group objectives and general methods for their attainment. This approach to personnel problems is largely impersonal.

Categories of potential trouble are identified, but they are kept in a purely neutral state and personalized only when they actually arise. This process results in a master template for your job.

The organizing function brings into play the manager's consideration of people in a more personal way. There are two recognized methods of structuring organizations: fitting people to particular job descriptions or tailoring job activities to the people you have available. The latter, of course, calls for more creativity in organizational planning. The superior manager strives diligently to arrive at a structure which will elicit the best qualities and efforts of the people reporting to him. He can give more latitude for each subordinate's creativity and innovation and can set more demanding goals on the basis of each one's strengths and depth of commitment. Many of the best and most functional organizations are based on this philosophy. The good manager does not begrudge the relatively large amounts of time required for setting up his organization. It is the vehicle by which his goals will be achieved, and the best results can be attained only by making full use of his human resources.

Another point worthy of note is the rapid and continuing increase in the use of the matrix type of organization. Here, a function is responsive to demands on its expertise from *any* part of the organization. In consequence, lines of authority become quite blurred; the accent is on responsibility and accountability to the entire enterprise. Thus the matrix organization is the most flexible type to use in these days of generally complex structures and interactions.

In the directing function, the actual interface between the manager's personality and those of his employees takes place. If there is going to be friction in the organization, it will occur here. Nowhere else is there greater need for you to know your people than in the day-to-day matters of directing. Managerial style assumes paramount importance in this part of your job. Douglas McGregor, in his concepts of Theory X and Theory Y, clearly reemphasized that people respond in the same vein in which they are approached.* If you trust them, they will return your trust in most cases; and the reverse is just as true.

The controlling function is fairly evenly divided between considerations of things and considerations of people. That is to say, we control our progress toward our objectives by means of reporting things through the activities of people. The manager must make a considered judgment about the number and kinds of controls with which he is going to burden his people. Whatever your decision in this area, it is well to remember how stultifying a mass of paperwork can be. It is depressingly easy to lose sight of the magic mountain of goals when struggling through the dead forest of largely meaningless controls. The trap is that each separate control can look (and even be) so beautifully logical and precise. But the accumulation of uncounted controls is certain death to the commitment and zest of your people. Every additional control with which you saddle them is further evidence of your basic distrust of them. You cannot expect them to have trust and confidence in you unless you demonstrate those attitudes toward them.

It is obvious that there are an infinite number of possible subdivisions of these four managerial functions. You

* Douglas McGregor, *The Human Side of Enterprise* (New York: McGraw-Hill Book Company, 1964).

can proliferate checks and balances against your performance until the entire procedure becomes sterile and meaningless. Only you can be the judge of how far you should break down the analytical procedure for the management of your job. However, you should listen to the comments of your superior, your peers, and your subordinates before you cast the final balance. Out of this exercise will obviously come some more inputs for your development program.

What's Ahead for You Now?

This analysis of your job as you see it is only the beginning. It will indicate the elements of a new development program aimed at catapulting you into an executive chair. There are two significant aspects of this plan which you may not have encountered before. First, the viewpoint and orientation will be both broader and deeper; second, any outside activities you may choose to participate in, such as professional seminars, institutes, and workshops, will be horribly expensive. Also, because some seminars are restricted to those who hold specified positions in the hierarchy, you might be in the rather delicate spot of having to request executive endorsement of your application to attend a particular seminar before you have had any overt indication from your top manager that you are being considered for another promotion. You should not feel embarrassed by this situation, since you are sincere in your efforts to better yourself and to prepare for greater responsibility.

If you are a typical middle manager, you are probably

plagued by myriad details in your daily work. It is going to take some doing to arrange your schedule so that you can attend some of these seminars. Of course, your plan to be absent from work implies that you have a capable understudy (or hopefully, two) to whom you can assign your responsibilities for a reasonable time.

Concurrently with attending formal institutes, you must make plans to enrich your present job. Although you may have to get clearance from your superior for much of this process, *you* are essentially the one involved in it. The enrichment of your job will, by its very nature, entail a similar enrichment of the assignments of your immediate subordinates. At this stage in the game, you cannot alter your job without involving theirs.

In looking ahead, you should be mentally and emotionally prepared for one thing: The wait for promotion to the executive level may be a long one. You are finally taking aim at the narrowest step in the company hierarchy, and vacancies at the executive level don't occur every second Tuesday. Contrary to a widely held belief, executives do not on the average die young. Moreover, a surprising large number of enterprises exempt their executives from the mandatory retirement age established for lower levels of management, so it is not uncommon to see many men in their seventies who are still actively in command of top-level jobs.

You will have to sublimate your anxiety about waiting for promotion by becoming engrossed in the twin pursuits of your present job and your new development plan. Both are important enough to absorb you almost completely, and they will help to allay your tensions.

There will be another repetitive item on your agenda:

the preparation of your family for another change in your situation. Your children will probably find the transition easier to make than will your wife. While the changes in your life will be largely job-centered, the changes in hers will be mostly social. From the time you announce your serious candidacy until you have actually been tapped for promotion, her position will be extremely difficult. She cannot make many overtures toward the wives of the executives without running the risk of being thought pushy. Yet neither can she ignore them and at the same time remain conscious of old loyalties and friendships. More than this, she will be caught in a pseudosocial relationship with some of the acquaintances you will be making as you expand your sphere of activity, even on your present job.

There is one more trap which you should be careful not to spring on yourself now. This is no time to be moving to a larger and more impressive home, no matter how desirable it might appear for family or other reasons. Such an action could only be taken amiss by those important people who are now watching your every move. The same warning goes for any lodges and country clubs to which you belong. Wait until your promotion has been announced officially before making any changes in these areas, or the boomerang effect might be fatal.

If you need an anxiety reducer, this might be an exceptionally good time for you to take on a new and intriguing hobby. It will absorb some of your excess adrenaline and reduce your anxiety by distracting your attention from your primary goal, if only for a few minutes at a time. You must recognize the ever present necessity for balance in your activities, both mental and physical. The pressures under which you live are increasing almost daily; you are the only one who can devise a viable method of containing them and retaining a semblance of normality in your life. This balance is critical to your health, and no one need tell you how important that is to you right now.

You would be fortunate if you could adopt a detached, almost Buddha-like attitude toward your job and life in general. If ever you have been in need of a protective shell, it is now. Maintain your general alertness, but avoid at all costs any debilitating distractions and extra worries.

1

Why Not Stay at Base Camp?

MANY of your acquaintances envy you your present position. Whether you are a department head or the manager of a group, they are awed by your position, power, status, and income. They make little if any distinction between a member of middle management and an executive. Perhaps they are vaguely aware that the executive gets more money and has a few extra privileges, but they can see no clear and basic difference between the two jobs.

Do You Really Know What You Already Have?

It is a human characteristic to undervalue the things with which we have become perfectly familiar. When you took your place in middle management you may actually have felt your power diminish, since in all probability fewer subordinates report to you directly now than did when you were a first- or second-line supervisor. The fact that you can make things happen over a wider and more complex area soon loses its novelty. Your office and physical surroundings are almost identical to those of your peers, and the fact that your office is significantly better than anything you had before is not important to you. The money? Frederick Herzberg* makes a good case for the proposition that a raise is a motivator for only one payday. Actually, you were briefly disturbed at how easily you became accustomed to the higher income and how quickly you again felt material needs.

As a middle manager, you make many big decisions every day as a regular part of your job. Moreover, the effect of these decisions on a major part of the enterprise is visible to the naked eye. But you are becoming increasingly perturbed because you are still not at a policy-making level, which is the really meaningful part of the organization's overall activities. Any contributions you make to the determination of company goals take the form of advice and counsel to the executive echelon, and you offer that only at their request.

The depth of your wish to make policy is one of the better barometers by which to judge your basic desire to become an executive. Many people find great satisfaction in the ability and authority to determine the direction for the entire organization. It is more an intellectual pleasure

* Frederick Herzberg, *The Motivation to Work* (New York: John Wiley & Sons, 1959).

than a sheer lust for power, and often it is not personalized at all as a means of self-actualization. It is a throwback to the feeling of the artisan who was responsible for conceiving and realizing an entire creative event. The concept of the whole is most satisfying to the man destined to become an executive.

Another benefit of your job as a middle manager is the noticeably widened circle of those outside your work group over whom you now exert an influence. Your position has brought you into focus for a large number of organization watchers, those for whom management people as a group have a continuing fascination. The fact that you are a responsible manager for a particular company automatically gives you status and esteem in their eyes; they listen to you and watch your moves with deep concentration. They are your public, as differentiated from the family of your working group.

The full realization of this situation comes as a shock to many new middle managers, who find it a source of uneasiness for a time. Actually, it should be ego bolstering within modest limits. Of course, it also restricts you, notably by curtailing some of your freedom to express your personal opinions openly to all listeners. Your slightest and most whimsical utterances have an influence far beyond any they ever enjoyed before; their potential for hurting you and the company is powerful.

Another of the good things you now enjoy is a much wider latitude in leading your immediate subordinates. Now that you are managing managers, you no longer have to observe the highly artificial limitations that were imposed on your relationships with subordinates when you were a first-line supervisor. In your attempts to build an effective management team, you can go in any direction that looks inviting or productive; in supervising the development of your replacements and the rest of your subordinates, you can employ any methods you find appealing. Unless your company has an extremely formal management development policy, you can study and apply the new tools as they are devised, keeping ever watchful for whatever effects they may produce. This is all to the good.

You can also use recently developed team procedures. If management by objectives appeals to you, feel free to introduce it into your part of the action, whether the rest of the enterprise has adopted it or not. Your segment is now large enough to allow you to rate results on a fairly objective basis. The same goes for many other modern management tools. In a nutshell, your power to innovate within your organization has been magnified many times, and it would be foolish not to take advantage of this fact.

Because you have much going for you as a middle manager, you should balance your present advantages against those you can see in the life of the executive, and come to a rational decision as to whether you want to relax and enjoy what you now have, or try for the next step. Anyone who tries to influence your decision (with the single exception of members of your family) is doing you no favor and should not be given your attention. This is true even of your boss, for he is a member of the executive team and many factors might influence any advice he tries to give you. There are occasions, of course, when he will be called upon for leadership of your activities, but this is not one of them.

*Are You Unable
to See Anything More in Your Job?*

If your answer to this question is in the affirmative, the chances against your being promoted again are very high. The moment you begin to find your present job a dead, immobile entity, you have to all intents begun to die in your career. Essentially, what this means is that your chances of going to the top level in the management of your enterprise are governed almost entirely by your attitude toward your present job. This is because your attitude will control your thinking, your actions, your interpersonal relationships, and your effect on everyone with whom you come in contact.

You have been lectured many times before about the importance of your attitude, but at this point it becomes crucial that you get the message. For example, how does the present turmoil among youth affect the way you regard the new young members of your workforce? Young people today are attacking our values. Some of them find it difficult or impossible to relate to the things we have long considered fundamental to our way of life. Unless you keep careful control of your own thinking, you will become hostile toward these new employees. If you seal them off, you are dead, for they are here to stay in the business world.

Your job is twofold: to reexamine your own values so as to be sure they are still what you thought them to be, and then to work with these young people to help them live with the realities of the world in which they are just beginning to operate. Yours is the greater responsibility,

19

since you are the one in charge. The fact that they question your leadership—or even reject it completely, at first—does not lessen your responsibility. Until you can come to some understanding with them, they will be dysfunctional in your organization, and everyone will suffer as a consequence.

If you have gradually come to see your present job as a finite, limited area, that attitude will affect your relationships with employees you have been working with for years. The change in your attitude will be perfectly apparent to them, and, since they recognize you as their leader, they will start to wonder whether their own values are out of step with those of the group. Your mental set is the strongest single determinant of your effectiveness, or lack of it, as a middle manager. It will make you or break you.

If you are doing an adequate or good job in the design and execution of your personal development program, there will be repeated stimuli which should help you to see your present position in a new light. If you have made a good choice of one of the new management tools to study, you can hardly fail to find some way of applying what you learn to your own work. The worst thing you could do at this time would be to fall victim to the middle management disease of resistance to change as a means of maintaining the status quo. It is true that the situation in which you are now working has been favorable to you and your progress, but that is not to say that it always will be. If you keep rigid in your outlook and practices while the entire world around you is changing, you will soon become ineffective as a manager.

At this particular point in your career, the best way of insuring your future promotability is to concentrate on your present job to the exclusion of everything else. Employ your best efforts as an analyst to look critically at your part of the action for constructive ways to modify it. Applying the methodology of the industrial engineer, hold each segment of your job up to valid criteria of worth, and be relentless in modifying or discarding any operation that fails to measure up. However, since discarding one method of operation entails its replacement by another, it is even more important that you make some careful judgments before you change any part of your routine.

The changes and personal growth you are now undergoing will be critical to your future success, no matter what your assignment. Whether you are promoted or not, you cannot hope to remain functional in your career unless you adjust to the changes that will come with increasing frequency every year of your life. The one factor you must not fail to recognize is the ever larger involvement of each segment of the business world with society at large. Your enterprise is an integral part of the entire social scene; its life or death depends on your ability, and that of the managers you work with, to sense what is going on in the world and to gear your business to respond to these changes, preferably as soon as they are established. This is not to say that you cannot innovate, or contribute to the changes, but whether you do or not your life as a modern manager will alter significantly.

Not the least of the critical elements in this whole process is the communication you owe your subordinates at every step of the way. Your success will of course be measured by your ability to make them aware of what is going on, of your plans to add to the system, or of any modifications you intend to make in those plans because

21

of external factors not subject to your control. Your people have a right to know what your plans are and to be given a lead time that is long enough for them to make the necessary adjustments without undue stress. They are entitled to the same consideration that you would like to have from your own superior.

Do You Want Big-Time Politics?

You could not have come as far as you have without some acquaintance with company politics. The chances are that you have made use of this device to help boost yourself into middle management, although this is not to say that the average middle manager gets his job through the deviousness of machine politics; those few who do are conspicuous for their rarity. But, on the other hand, there are few who do not owe something of their advancement to concerted political activity. There might even at this moment be a small coterie of your special friends who operate as a political unit for their mutual benefit. So it's more than likely that you know something of the pressures such people can exert when they work as a group on strategic spots in the organization. So long as personal and group integrity are maintained, there can be no opprobrium attached to such forms of company politics. You are conforming to established practice.

Of one thing you may be certain: You have never yet seen company politics played with the intensity and for the high stakes you will experience if you seriously seek promotion to the executive ranks. This intensity is understandable, since the competitors will indeed be the cream of the crop, the ambitious, strong, take-charge, most intelligent members of the managerial group. Their drive is significantly greater than that of their peers. They want the big job to the exclusion of any other personal goals. They are willing to go to extremes in effort, sacrifice, and planning to attain their ends. They are much smoother and less blatant in their political operations. They become terribly proficient at hiding the ball and deceiving the observer. Many of their power plays are executed on the order of a difficult three-cushion billiard shot, with the final objective of knocking out a competitor. Their play is for keeps. One of the most pitiful sights in industry is a contender taken out by one of these ploys without even realizing clearly what has happened to him.

There is a rough sort of justice in this situation, even if it is Machiavellian. The candidate's choice of political group is one of the many tests of his judgment to which he will be put before he gets where he wants to be. From now on, it is going to be more important every day for you to be able to size up people quickly and with a high degree of accuracy. Unless you can do this consistently, you have no business in the big leagues. And the most important aspect of this is your ability to predict how people will react to a given situation. Of course, this is much harder to do with people you know only casually than it is with those you work with every day.

The number one rule you have to keep in mind always is that the political debts you incur along the way are in the form of IOUs, and they are undated. For every favor received, you will owe one of equal magnitude, and you must pay up on presentation of the demand note by your debtor. This can become extremely awkward, but it is the law of the game. What we are saying is never commit yourself beyond your willingness to repay.

Of course, during this process you will also be accruing credits. Some people will make demands upon you before you have received anything from them, and if you grant these favors, you have one coming from them in exactly the same way. Over a long time period, these debits and credits will balance out fairly well, if you have any skill at the play.

You will do far better if you play your politics as a loner. Do *not* involve your people in this activity. If you drag them in unwillingly, you will ultimately incur their enmity. Of course, if they offer their services and cooperation, you can either accept gratefully or reject gracefully, according to your judgment of their true motives and their ability to give you a hand. You have every right to the services of trusted lieutenants, if their offer is bona fide and they can contribute something.

At this point, we should remove the shadow of cynicism from the past few paragraphs. All the statements have been made with faith in your basic honesty and goodwill. If these are ever in serious doubt, your prognosis is extremely poor, and your future is shrouded in deepest black. You learned long ago that your attitude in your career must be one of hard realism, backed by impeccable honesty. The honest man cannot always win, especially if his rival is another honest man, but at least he can lose with his head high and with no disturbance to his sleep at night.

The one overpowering danger you face is that of becoming so engrossed in the game of politics that you forget the really important criteria for your upcoming advancement, such as doing your job to the best of your ability.

Your ability to do your job exceptionally well, and still to have the time and energy to get involved in other activities, will be the standard against which you will be measured. From now on, your signal is *not* to keep your eye on the ball, but to watch and evaluate the entire field.

How Much More Power Do You Need?

An odd change appears in the power differential when a man moves from middle management to the executive level. There can be no question, of course, that the executive has greater power than the middle manager within the organization; yet curiously it seems at first that he loses, rather than gains, power by his elevation. There are two reasons for this. First, he probably now has fewer people reporting to him directly than he did as a middle manager. Second, since his power is dispersed throughout the organization, and deals in the main with policy formation, it becomes depersonalized. In addition, the executive's strength is relatively invisible; the middle manager, in contrast, sees a significant portion of the enterprise in action from day to day and has immediate and real power over that portion.

Another aspect of the middle manager's power, and one which is often overlooked, is the considerable influence he builds up in the rest of the industry and the outside community, especially if he has been high on the totem pole of middle management for an extended period of time. It is not at all uncommon for such a man to be visibly more prestigious than a newly promoted executive who has not had time to establish himself in his job. Thus the manager who has a strong power drive may find more satisfaction in his current position than in the relative obscurity of an executive position.

The middle manager who is trying to decide whether he wants to advance further should consider carefully another important fact: An unending power struggle goes on among executives, especially in larger companies where there are many executive positions or more than one executive echelon. It is all but impossible to predict how a man will react to this pressure. Some find it challenging, even invigorating, while others are immediately aware of insupportable tension. It is for this reason that we restate the question which is the theme of this segment: How much more power do you need? This is one of the key points on which your personal decision should rest. If your appetite for power is nearly insatiable, you will know the answer. If you have any doubt about it, you should recheck many other factors before you make a firm announcement of your candidacy for the final promotion. The decision is of too much importance to your mental and physical well-being to be treated lightly.

One of the most important evaluations you must make is whether there is a low, medium, or high probability that you will undergo an actual personality change upon accession to the big time. We have all seen harrowing examples of men whose characters underwent a complete reversal when they came into positions of power. This is the greatest career wrecker anyone can ever have the misfortune to experience and should be avoided by all possible means.

The basic assumption of this discussion is that you will always exercise your power benignly, for the benefit of the most people, and in no case purely for your personal aggrandizement. The latter is, of course, intolerable, and always will be. The greater the power, the greater the duty to those over whom that power is exercised. Value judgments take on added importance, as does each decision the manager makes. Since you get your work done through other people, and thereby make your reputation and have your chance for personal success and recognition, you owe special consideration to those who have put you where you are.

Another ongoing and inescapable concomitant of your power is your duty to carry out your responsibilities in the best interests of the enterprise at all times. The balancing act between duty to subordinates and duty to the company can become extremely troublesome unless you maintain your mental health and hone your powers of decision to a fine edge. Remember, as an executive your skills at conceptualization will constantly be at a premium. Your performance will be judged almost exclusively on your ability to see the big picture with reference to the men, money, and materials at your disposal.

Making the decision of how much power you need is entirely a personal matter. Most assuredly, you should remove yourself from the distractions of the daily job while you are wrestling this problem to a decision. You owe it to yourself, your people, and your enterprise to concentrate with everything in you while you are weighing the factors involved in your ultimate decision and bending every effort to be fair to all concerned. The man who finally comes up with a negative answer to the question of advancement to the executive level has probably rendered the finest service to his company.

Can You Stand Total Isolation?

Our whole society is based on man's fundamental need to interact with and live with others. The man who chooses to operate alone is called a loner and is looked upon with suspicion by his fellow men. Yet top-level leaders in the business world are forced to operate much of the time completely alone, without even counsel and guidance from another person. This isolation derives partly from the group and partly from the decision of the executive himself. Chances are that he has been chosen for some special qualities, either native or carefully developed. One of these is a better-than-average ability to observe the scene around him and forecast, with a high probability of accuracy, what will occur in the future that will affect his work group. For this task, as for others, he must be almost completely self-reliant, because no one else can be of much help to him in making these judgments. He may or may not like it, but this is one aspect of his job that will be with him as long as he is a leader.

You have had intimations of this state of isolation during your work in middle management, but its full force has never hit you. Some men cannot adjust to it and for that reason are unsuccessful as executives. Isolation can play queer tricks on human personality. It has a way of accentuating individual quirks, and some of them may suddenly become obtrusive, to the detriment of the executive. For example, he may become increasingly distrustful and even paranoid about his associates' motivations and intentions toward him. Or he may begin to underestimate the strengths of his competitors and to think of himself as omniscient and invulnerable. Either of these neurotic tendencies will of course work strongly against him and must be guarded against if he wants to make it on the new job.

Certain religious groups advocate and use the retreat for meditation. As a prospective executive, you might do well to try this once or twice, just to see how you react to being totally alone for a few days. Of course, in such a short time you will not necessarily find out how well you can handle a semipermanent isolation, but you are likely to learn something about your reactions to being alone.

The isolation of the executive is also dangerous to his communications system. Unless he remains on the alert at all times, he may miss cues of extreme importance to his operations or may work under false assumptions which can be fatal to his plans for the group. In most cases, the executive must make a special effort to set up a communications network which will automatically feed him signals from his surroundings. He dare not trust to luck for his informational inputs, or he will be quickly and irrevocably down the drain. This procedure is further complicated by the fact that he cannot go out seeking his information, because his respondents would try to tell him what they think he wants to hear rather than what he should hear.

Furthermore, because the executive operates in a near vacuum, it becomes especially difficult for him to make judgments about the new people he meets and comes to associate with. The old familiar sources of information he had about newcomers when he was a middle manager will become largely inoperative, and he will be left more and more to judge for himself the intentions and actions of others. This can make it quite difficult to expand his circle of acquaintances and friends, thereby limiting his personal growth.

Merely naming and identifying these results of job isolation will not necessarily prepare you for their effect upon you. Your mental health has never been more important to you, and it will continue to be important as long as you occupy the executive chair. One of the more obvious types of preventive therapy is to seek out and cultivate the associations you will naturally have with your peers in other enterprises. These social contacts will be more meaningful than will dealings with members of your own group. By comparing notes with your peers, you will get a chance to repair and maintain your perspective about what is going on in your own environment. This is of the utmost importance to you, obviously.

Unless you are particularly careful, your posture of aloneness can carry over into your family life, and the results could be particularly painful. If your wife and children come to the conclusion that you are withdrawing from them, their natural defensive reaction would be to withdraw from you. Many men can adjust to being alone on the job, but no normal person can tolerate being isolated in his own home. Since you cannot really expect your family to understand fully the nature of your new executive job and its demands on you, you must assure them that you will not become isolated from them at home. This will be difficult for your wife to accept, especially if you have been used to discussing some aspects of your job with her. Now, as an executive, you will find that most of the interesting facets of your work must remain classified, even at home. Your helpmate will have to be made to understand that your apparent uncommunicativeness is not indicative of a change in your relationship with her. This will take a little doing, but it is imperative.

If ever you have needed strong familial ties, now is the time. They can be strongly supportive if you are assiduous in tending them.

How Many of Your Friends Do You Need to Keep?

There is another good aspect of your job as a middle manager of which you have been made aware many times. That is the comfortable, solid, and satisfying personal friendships you have developed on the job over the years. Your friends have gone to bat for you frequently, both individually and as a group, and have contributed greatly to your success as a manager. They have accepted and reinforced your critical decisions—which has had its effect on upper management—and have turned down opportunities to take advantage of your errors. Thus the entire climate in which you now work is in no small part a result of their attitudes and actions.

The moment it becomes known that you are an active candidate, even a possibility, for promotion to the executive level, this happy situation will begin to change subtly. These people are your friends, but they are also human beings. It is (except in the most unusual men) too much to expect that their attitude toward you will not be altered. You are about to leave the group, and they will start, with varying degrees of swiftness, the process of sealing you off from what has been a sort of club. In some of them the dominant emotion will be pure jealousy, which is always accompanied by hostility and usually by aggressive action. In other words, they will transform you from a friend into an enemy, and you can count on them no more. Others in the group will not be jealous, but will start to encase you in the vague mistrust people always feel toward their Olympian superiors. It will be especially unfortunate if your new title is vice-president. Even though you are only one step removed from them, you will become in their eyes a member of a different race whose thinking, mores, and responses they do not understand. They will not feel animosity toward you; they will simply cease to understand you, and you will be removed from their circle of friends.

The complement to this development will be the changes in your own intellectual and emotional life. You will no doubt assure yourself often that your feelings toward your friends will not change. This is simply not a realistic expectation. As you see some of the people who were close to you develop antagonistic attitudes, you would be less (or more) than human if you did not react in a similar manner. Your reaction may be less severe than theirs, since you are the one whose lot is to be bettered, but you will undergo some change.

From the time you become a serious candidate for an executive position, you can also expect changes to occur in your relationships with your immediate subordinates. Most of these changes you will initiate yourself because you know that there will be another level of management between you and them, and this is certain to affect your relationship with them. As a professional practitioner of good management, you will realize that your subordinates will soon have a new boss, and that you must do nothing to upset the relationship which they will develop with him.

A recognizable degree of estrangement will grow between you and your people, regardless of how genuinely glad they may be about your continued success and how much they know they have contributed to it.

These changes are inevitable; however, since you generated many of the changes yourself, you can take some preventive steps to keep the schism from becoming disruptively deep. One of the better ways is to discuss, on an informal one-to-one basis, the expected change in your position. Once your subordinates understand the process, they will tend to be much more forgiving of the alterations they see in your operation. They are managers like yourself, and can be expected to understand what is happening to you.

It would be an exaggeration to imply that you will lose all the friendships and good associations which you have enjoyed in your managerial career simply because you are going to be promoted once more. There are always those who will remain completely steadfast and rocklike in their friendship for you. You will have to classify these among your fringe benefits and be properly thankful for them. These people will also form the center of the communications network you will organize as you enter your new position. Their action will be one of the buffers against the isolation you will experience. It is to be hoped that you will be able to count on this core of true friends to help you maintain a realistic perspective when you move upstairs. To this group of people, your door should literally always be open.

*　　*　　*

This chapter has asked you to examine your present

situation in great depth, with special attention to the advantages you now enjoy. Even though you are on the threshold of an exciting promotion, it is imperative that you still be able to see ways of expanding your present job. Unless you can do so, you are not a real candidate for the executive level.

You must also be prepared for the quantum escalation of the politically pressured atmosphere of the higher echelon. That, and the power plays in which you will be involved, will provide either much of your personal tension or most of the excitement and challenge of your life as an executive. You should also examine and attempt to evaluate your ability to operate in a near vacuum, because you will experience an isolation you have never known before.

Finally, you must deal with the significant disruptions and upsetting changes in your personal relationships with your subordinates as you get ready for promotion to the executive rank.

2

Do You Know
What It's Like at the Top?

THE interfaces with top management which you have as a middle manager, although undeniably many more than you had as a first- or second-line supervisor, are delusive in nature. With the single exception of your own executive boss, you meet the members of the group in situations only marginally related to the job. As part of your development program, your supervisor has probably sent you upstairs to make presentations or to represent him at his boss's staff meetings. These contacts, if we even label them as such, are so transitory as to be of little use in teaching you how the executives operate. Moreover, they have probably put you under rather severe stress during these encounters, which lessened your ability to form valid opinions about them. We have assumed, perhaps wrongly, that your boss is himself an executive. If your enterprise is large, you, as a member of middle management, may be reporting to another member of middle management one echelon higher than you, rather than to someone on the executive level.

We have already explored the nearly total isolation within which most executives operate. This is partly a function of their job design and partly a result of their own decision. The latter aspect has a perfectly predictable result: Most executives tend to be uncommunicative in their casual contacts with you. The two exceptions are the occasion when you receive a specific assignment from them and are obliged to report to them about it, and the occasion when they seek you out in order to evaluate you and your potential.

This highly unsatisfactory relationship between you and the executives makes it difficult for you to conceptualize their job. Your intelligence and training make you rebel at the thought of accepting secondhand stories concerning the habits and *modus operandi* of top management, yet you find yourself repeatedly frustrated by your inability to develop a clear picture of how they function. A situation of this sort will naturally present a challenge to you. The best way to throw some light on the problem is to make discreet inquiries of your friends in middle management who are old-timers in the company. Their store of accumulated experience and sensitivity will give you a better background for your personal observations and experiences.

In other words, you will have established some bench marks for comparison.

Another source seldom thought of is *Who's Who,* if the executive in question is listed there. Since the nominees for entry write their own biographical sketches, it is often possible to get fine insights into their personalities and backgrounds by reading what they have to say about themselves. Even the canniest of us become quite artless when talking about ourselves.

How Real Are Your Contacts
with the Executive Level?

Another sad fact has to be reported. In his deviousness, the executive may deliberately set out to leave a wrong impression with you in your contacts with him. He may have an ax to grind and want to start a rumor through you as a trial balloon to test the wind. Or he may be playing devil's advocate and looking for insight into your particular set of values and operating philosophy. You would be wrong to infer from this that you should never trust a member of your top management, but the question, What did he mean by that? should always be in your mind. It will be your best guide in casual and unstructured contacts with the executives of your enterprise, at least until you join their ranks. Remember, most of their business is done with their peers or opposite numbers in other firms, rather than with the middle managers in their own companies.

One fact you must keep in mind: The executive is

chosen at least in part because of his continued *positive* deviation from the norms of your company. The leader must be different from his people, at least in his ability to be a step or so in front of the pack, and he must also be able to sense changes and trends more quickly than do those who follow him. You may find it hard at first to reconcile yourself to the necessity of being recognizably different from those around you, but it is a prime requisite for being named to membership on the executive team.

Everyone realizes the artificiality of the special or company occasions when you will be thrown in with members of top management. Dinners, anniversary parties, award presentations, and other events are by their very nature unlike the day-to-day activities of the average executive. In these situations, he is making a conscious effort at internal public relations; he is the politician incarnate, and any similarity to his ordinary personality is purely coincidental. He has his own special cache of clichés and platitudes reserved for these occasions, and he doctors them so that they will seem fresh and palatable to the assemblage. The man who grows lyrical at the banquet over the merits of safety may growl fiercely at spending $100 for a machine guard in the plant. This should come as no surprise to you, since you have seen the technique used many times before.

You will be fortunate if you occasionally meet some of the executives off the job. They are likely to be more relaxed and under less pressure to play whatever role they judge pertinent to their position. When you meet them in church, in service clubs, or on the golf course, you will have a much better chance to make a meaningful evaluation of them as individuals and as executives.

What Goes On in Those Top-Secret Meetings?

One of the most frustrating aspects of the life of the middle manager is his awareness of the great number of mysterious meetings which take place on mahogany row. If your office is situated so that you see some of the comings and goings, you are aware that many of those who attend these meetings are total strangers to you and that some of them are obviously not employees of your company. The meetings may go on for hours, with no interruptions save the possible entry and exit of a secretary with files as they are called for, and the breaks for coffee.

The maddening thing about these meetings is that your boss will never even mention them to you, let alone communicate anything of their content or significance. You feel exactly like a stepchild at these times, and unless you are careful there may be an adverse effect on your attitude and morale. You tell yourself that there are many reasons why total security must be maintained regarding these meetings. The planning done at the top echelon is of a long-range nature; implementation may be scheduled for three to five years downstream. Huge amounts of money are involved, as well as new products, changes in marketing strategy, and many other things which your competition is dying to learn.

It does little good to remind yourself that being excluded from these events—or from knowing about them—is not a sign of your superior's lack of trust in you. He is simply operating on the well-known fact that security for any given information always exists in inverse proportion to the number of people who know it. The calculated decision to restrict information about a particular subject is part of the job of every manager. You do the same thing yourself when you withhold information from your subordinates which you feel they do not need to know.

This philosophy is currently under heavy attack in the business world. Many theorists now maintain that dozens of facts are kept secret at each level which could be known further down the hierarchy without harm. In fact, management sometimes makes itself look ridiculous by going to great lenghs to stop the spread of information which is already public property, such as data published routinely in the annual report. Psychologically, you are running a high risk of severely demotivating your subordinates every time they know you are suppressing information. Furthermore, the manager's attitude about secrecy can boomerang savagely because of the current prevalence of industrial espionage. The fact being ruthlessly kept from your own people may already be known to your competition through a leak in your organization. It would be better if you were reluctant *not* to pass on a piece of information to your subordinates.

Another reason for an apparently secret meeting at the top level may be that the topic has nothing to do with company business. Executives as a matter of course become deeply involved in the work of their professional associations or in community affairs. They may hesitate to reveal that they are holding meetings relating to those activities during company time and for this reason may fail to keep you informed.

Also, the isolation in which the executive works may cause him to be less communicative than is necessary. Then, having become accustomed to his solitary ways and having failed to communicate, he finds it extremely difficult to elicit the information he needs from below. He then may become resentful and intensify his own uncommunicativeness, and the vicious circle is perpetuated. If you can imprint this situation thoroughly on your consciousness while you are still in middle management and move into the executive circle aware that this fault is to be avoided at all costs, you will start your new job with a big advantage over your peers.

Of course, it would be grossly unfair to imply that *no* meetings at the top level should be kept secret. As mentioned, in many industries the nature of a new product must be kept from the competition until the last possible moment so as to preserve an advantage in the field. Likewise, certain financial negotiations cannot be made public until their consummation is assured, or they may never be consummated. Major organizational restructurings have a right time and a wrong time for being made known; if they are prematurely publicized, the effects on personnel may be devastating, with a concomitant loss of some people you need to keep. Similarly, the evolution of a major shift in company philosophy or policy must be kept secret until everything has been firmed up, or the entire enterprise may be put in jeopardy over the controversy which will be generated by discussion at all levels. These are the parts of the executive's responsibility that are peculiarly and personally his, and he has every right—even duty—to keep his own counsel until the final decisions have been made.

For your mental health, your attitude toward these closed meetings should be kept loose and easy. Shrug them off, and operate under the assumption that you have the full trust and confidence of your superior and that he will continue to furnish you with the information you need to do your job. You can thus avoid a full-blown neurosis which will complicate your life at the new level and make your adjustment more difficult. There will be enough to keep you busy without letting your own actions and thoughts upset you. The physical energy you will save can carry you over many of the initial bumps with less disruption and trauma.

Do You Know the Difference Between Tactics and Strategy?

One of the distinguishing characteristics of the executive's job is the long time span between the planning and execution of his actions. When you were a first-line supervisor, your decisions dealt with the problems of the moment. Now, as a middle manager, your decisions cover a time span of a few months or at most a year. When you become an executive, the time increments of your work will be three, five, or even ten years. This is because you will then be planning and executing strategy for the entire enterprise, rather than tactics to overcome the immediate obstacle.

A brilliant *tactician* can look good while reacting instantaneously to an emergency. He is a fire fighter and has no time to consider his actions and their possible effects. His job is to meet the challenge of the moment. The good *strategist,* on the other hand, must concern himself with his competitor's master plan and must devise ways to circumvent *his* actions. He must consider both defensive and offensive positions. If he is to win, his evaluations of the strengths and weaknesses of his own position and that of his challenger must be impeccable. It is for this reason that the executive will be judged finally and definitively upon his ability to conceptualize—on his skill and accuracy in looking at the big picture.

Some people make an effort to clothe this activity in mystery. They would like you to think that the ability to conceptualize is a special attribute possessed by few people, and that if you weren't born with it, you should forget about it. This is completely untrue. Any normally intelligent person can be trained to conceptualize. Most people have to reorient their thinking to acquire this skill, but you have changed your ways of thinking several times before. The key is to be able to see relationships between facts which appear dissimilar on the surface. You are working with the geometry of your business activities.

The modern business scene is no longer the happy hunting ground for the brilliant, daring entrepreneur that it was a generation or so ago. True, there are still a few geniuses who become immensely successful on the strength of solo operations. But in the main, the modern executive does far better to master and use the many new tools at his disposal and to work with a carefully selected and highly trained team of associates. The day of the science of management is just around the corner; the contributions of the artist to the field are becoming less and less important to the overall operation and will eventually be used almost entirely for decorative or esthetic effects.

The solid, day-to-day efforts of the executive will be increasingly concerned with such tools as operations research which he now has at his command and with the new techniques being introduced at a bewilderingly rapid rate. All these will contribute to the executive's planning and execution of his strategy; he will stand or fall on his ability to make them work for him and his team. Thus you must prepare yourself to make an immediate adjustment to strategic operation when you become an executive. You will be allowed too little phase-in time to let you make a leisurely changeover. The day you are confirmed in your new position you will become a strategist rather than a tactician, and you will remain so from there on out.

You will have one thing going for you. You will be given much more latitude in picking your subordinates as an executive than you had as a manager at lower levels in the hierarchy. You can change the configuration of the organization considerably by your choice of subordinates and your rearrangement of responsibilities. If you are truly ready to be named an executive, you will certainly know whom you can work with comfortably. You will be aware of special strengths which can make just the right contributions to the satisfaction of your group's needs. Actually, the planning of your staffing efforts is the first step in your overall strategy and will set the tone of your operation for a long time to come.

Oddly enough, as an executive you will feel the pressures of time more strongly than you ever have before. By that we mean not only the pressures of everyday work, but also the time pressures of your long-range decisions, which will be with you every minute. Those five-year deadlines looming over you can become nearly intolerable.

The difference between the mental set of the strategist and that of the tactician will become one of your more serious working problems. Your middle managers may be blinded to the objectives of the policy you hand to them to implement because of the apparent immediate disadvantages in terms of their present work. It will be up to you to convince them of the viability of your proposals and to elicit their cooperation in putting your strategy into effect. You will not be able to do this singlehandedly; you are one step too far removed from the action, and you must rely on your staff to see that the work is really done.

All this means that the most necessary weapon of the successful executive is his self-confidence. You cannot afford to have major doubts about your planning. There will be enough of that exhibited by your subordinates; you must believe in yourself. Naturally, your confidence must be buttressed by meticulous work and long, hard study. You can't afford to leave out of consideration anything that is germane to the problem, and your judgmental and evaluative powers must be honed to a fine edge as you prepare to justify your self-confidence to the enterprise and the rest of the industry. Because of the magnitude of the risks you will be taking, you will be allowed few errors.

Do You Dream of Making Innovations?

You may never before have been required to be an innovator. Chances are that when you were a first-line supervisor, you were discouraged from doing anything radically new. Many managers feel distrustful and insecure when faced with the prospect of launching a new venture. When you became a middle manager, pressures from all directions discouraged any ideas you had which took you out of the established course. Now, however, the situation will change as you enter an executive position. Any enterprise which has the slightest hope of remaining competitive—let alone improving its position—has thoroughly absorbed one fact of life: You can survive only if you are the first with the best, which probably will include proliferation and diversification of products. If you are to succeed at the policy-making level, you will have to make your fair share of contributions to these conditions of change.

This does not mean that you will have to make a momentous discovery or hatch a world-beating invention every second Tuesday. Rather, your procedure will be to cultivate a sensitivity for the market life of your present bread-and-butter items and to insure that they will be followed by an orderly series of replacements. In other words, you should adopt the working method of the industrial engineer: Be constantly on the alert for the possible advantages of different combinations of existing things. Rearrangement can be as new and inviting as a completely novel product, and innovation can be as welcome and as profitable in the realms of engineering, manufacturing, quality assurance, and marketing as it is in the product area.

The quest for the new and different can be pursued in several directions. First, you must continually cultivate a sensitivity to cues fed to you by your environment. What are your customers looking for? What does the buying public at large demand from its vendors at this particular time? Have you observed excess capacity at present not utilized by your manufacturing people? Second, you must maintain a constantly inquiring and prodding attitude toward those around you. Many of them will have ideas germane to your problem, but it is highly unlikely that they will volunteer these ideas without your encouragement. Thus your position will be primarily that of a catalyst rather than a creator. Your job will be to expedite and facilitate reactions which would eventually occur by themselves. As these points indicate, you will be the keystone in the arch leading toward your company's continued health and prosperity. Any enterprise in which the executive level does not cultivate this awareness is moribund.

One profitable developmental gambit at this point would be to conduct a planned survey of the general condition of your industry. We all tend toward tunnel vision if we remain too closely focused on our immediate job responsibilities. Right now might be a good time to take a few weeks from your job and make contact with both the other members of your field and the customers whom all of you service. This is the equivalent of the brainstorming sessions you have sometimes used internally. The important thing is to keep your mind completely open and suspend judgment until you have gathered all the pertinent data. The necessary winnowing, evaluating, and establishing of priorities should be done only after a proper period of gestation of the ideas presented to you.

There is an overriding constraint to this entire activity which must never be forgotten. Newness for the sake of newness is completely sterile, and change for the sake of change is indefensible. Any innovations you introduce into your operations will have to be defended vigorously against all critics.

Concurrent with all this activity, you must keep in the back of your mind the psychological effects on your people every time you implement a change of any magnitude. You might become so absorbed in the brilliance of your new project that you forget the trauma always associated with a major change. The way to handle this problem is, of course, to maintain functional communication with your subordinates at all times. Change is never resisted if the rationale for it is clear and well understood. Those who work for you will never altogether forgive you if you fail them at this critical juncture. Keep them on your side by taking them thoroughly into your confidence at the earliest possible moment—and this almost always means before the go, no-go decision has been solidified.

An apparent digression is in order here to take stock of some of the necessary changes in your present assignment. The developmental program to prepare you for entry into the executive circle will necessitate some impressive rearrangements of your current job life. Actually, the outcome will be completely salutary if you take full advantage of the situation, because the alterations involved will be definitive in indicating the proper person to replace you when you are promoted. In a sense, it is a trial by combat for the competitors for your succession. The extra performance reviews entailed will be well repaid as they put into perspective the relative positions of your staff members. This does not mean that you are obligated to name a replacement from your own staff, but the odds are that you will. And if no satisfactory candidate appears, you are in one sense subject to criticism for an imperfect job of training along the way. There is more of the teacher to the job of the manager than any other single element. The critical thing for you right now is to broaden your perspective. Remember to take a critical look at your conceptual abilities.

*How Good Are You
in National and World Economics?*

As an executive, you will be required for the first time
to have some degree of expertise in economics. You cannot do successful planning for your enterprise unless you
are able to forecast economic trends with reasonable accuracy. This is true whether or not your part of the action
includes finance. The interrelationships among finance,
engineering, manufacturing, and marketing are so close at
the executive level that they cannot be separated into discrete entities.

To say you need to become knowledgeable in economics does not mean that you will have to get a degree
from a recognized college of finance. Attention to economics has become increasingly common in industry in
the past few years, and there are many good seminars on
finance for the nonfinancial executive. With one or two of
these as a port of embarkation, you can navigate the sea of
knowledge you must acquire. The literature in the area is
voluminous; your chore will be to winnow out the writings
most meaningful for your needs. It goes without saying
that you should take the time to scan *The Wall Street
Journal* thoroughly every day and read the articles which
promise to be helpful. Many managers fail to take full advantage of the statistical services offered by the national
trade associations of most industries. You might also
wish to become acquainted with one of the more promi-
nent economists in a nearby university, even if it is necessary to pay him a consultant fee for his services.

You need not become a slave to this new aspect of your

prospective job. You should become closely familiar with the précis furnished you daily by one of your staff subordinates. Let his fingers do the walking through the plethora of words.

If you are a neophyte in the field of economics, you will be disturbed at first by the lack of accord among the so-called experts. In fact, it is not at all uncommon to read two diametrically opposed forecasts by theorists of nearly equal reputation about the economic future. You might find it helpful simply to determine which economist seems to be in favor with a plurality of the businessmen you respect and to cast your lot with his thinking until he is proved wrong. If this seems disturbingly similar to Russian roulette, remember that economics is too inexact a science for any one person even to approach infallibility. Your responsibility is to follow as closely as you can the man you think to be the best of the theorists, make the necessary judgments concerning your operation as quickly as possible, and implement indicated changes promptly and with finesse.

The key is never to be late in whatever corrective or anticipatory action you have decided upon. Here, too, time is of the essence. Remember, however, that the time spans of personal economic forecasts for your industry and your enterprise will usually be made in five- or ten-year increments. Major changes in your company in the areas of finance, manufacturing, and marketing are not implemented overnight. Sufficient lead time must be given to allow for smooth and untroubled adjustment.

It should be obvious from the foregoing that close integration of your efforts with those of others at the executive level is critical. More than one company has been completely wrecked because two high-level managers went in opposite economic directions without communicating with each other. Economic decisions for the entire company must be a team effort, although the chief executive is naturally responsible for the final decision. Of utmost urgency is your responsibility to feed clean and uncontaminated data from your area of jurisdiction into the action center.

One aspect of your overall responsibility in the area of economics might be easy to overlook: You must communicate closely with your subordinates, both about your economic thinking and about the decisions you reach. They should never be forced to work in the dark in these matters. Their inputs will be much more definitive if they know the general ground rules of the game. This is a universal truth in management, but its importance in economic matters is of the life-or-death variety. Since so many new executives come to the job as unsophisticated in economics as you will, no criticism can be leveled at you for seeking counsel repeatedly in these matters. Make full use of the elders and the wise men in your enterprise for guidance.

The fundamental principle involved here is simple: Learn your way around in economics as a body of knowledge, and apply what you learn to relevant aspects of your job, but try to keep this new element as uncomplicated as you can, both for your sake and the company's.

A fascinating primrose path leads off from this facet of your executive job. You have probably been investing money in the market personally for several years. But the chances are that you have allocated your "gambling money" to this activity and have in the main turned it over to a broker to handle, keeping only the loosest control over the actual buying and selling. Now, when you begin to feel a growing sophistication in the area of economics, you may want to run your own ship in the stock market. At best, this is a dangerous ploy, for two reasons. First, you have *not* miraculously become a financial wizard; second, absorption in the intricacies of stock market trading can rob you of too much valuable time which you could spend more profitably on the basic aspects of your job. Far better that you leave your gambling in the hands of your broker and forget about it until income tax time.

What's Your Stake in the Company?

At this point, you will have to redetermine the exact extent of your personal involvement in the enterprise. If you accept a promotion to the executive level, you will greatly magnify your responsibility to the company, since your share of the load will now encompass a significant part of the total assets. Your success or failure will be clearly visible in the lower right-hand corner of the balance sheet. At the same time, you will of course get a large increase in pay and possibly some deferred benefits such as vested retirement or stock options. Perhaps you will find yourself modestly wealthy overnight.

These considerations can hardly fail to have a major effect on your thinking and actions. Should you want to move to another company, you would find it more difficult from the executive level than from the middle management level. Unless you are to be the chief executive, there is always a shadow of suspicion attached to a lateral transfer of an executive from one company to another. Even though you might see a much greater challenge and opportunity in making such a move, the observer who did not know all the facts would wonder how you had fouled up your last assignment. This could have a negative effect on your interpersonal relationships in your new affiliation. If you make the move as a result of an executive search discovery, the chances are good that some of your new associates will have a clouded picture of your entry.

The ties that accompany a promotion to the top echelon will tend to bind you more strongly to the organization which gave you the opportunity to share the top rung. When you find yourself in this situation, you will experience a concomitant increase in the emotion with which you follow the ups and downs of your firm. What is good for business is good for you, and vice versa. With increasing personalization of all your business activities will come a threat to your mental and physical health, unless you take some firm precautions. From here on out, you should never miss a vacation or an opportunity to take a few days or a few hours off for a change of pace. The objective of all your activity is to keep yourself mentally young. The moment your mind becomes set and unchangeable, you are through. If you discover that this is your position, you should liquidate your assets and make plans for retirement. Only the young in mind and spirit have any chance of beating the industrial jungle to a standstill and maintaining their place in it. We should reinforce here the earlier suggestion that you take on some new hobbies. They are great for providing good mental stimulation and sometimes the physical exercise you might otherwise be missing.

Years ago, when you first became fascinated with the

idea of becoming a supervisor, you discovered the value of discreet introspection. In the intervening time you have probably become fairly adept at this art and have made it an integral part of your life. It is at this point in your career that this will now start to pay you handsome dividends. Of course, it is to be hoped that you have also cultivated a sense of balance, so that you will exercise moderation; it would be unfortunate if you developed a neurosis about your mirror watching.

In reality, this deeper sense of involvement is your big chance to complete your maturation into a truly fine and competent manager. As you prove your ability to take on a heavier load, you will clear the last great hurdle in your career race. From here on in, it's a flat course. Speed will still be a requisite, but some of the former pressures will have been mitigated. Keep firing but do it on target, and conserve your ammunition.

*   *   *

This chapter has asked you to take a look at how much you really know about the job of the executive, and to help you to decide whether you want it after all.

In the first place, you will realize that your previous contacts with executives have been rather sketchy. There has been an air of unreality about them which probably disturbs you now. Part of this has been deliberate, since many executives are in the habit of creating ambiguity about their actions, even with their direct subordinates. This is because they feel vulnerable if they are too easily and clearly read by those with whom they associate. This same aura of mystery will surround some of their most mundane activities, and this again will be by design, for the same reason.

As you entertain the prospect of another promotion, you must learn to differentiate between tactics (at which you are now a master) and strategy (at which you are still a neophyte). This will require that you reorient your thinking and adopt a new mental set.

For the first time in your career, your associates will not only expect, but demand, that you become a masterful innovator, since innovation is a major function of any executive. But the innovations you will actually push through to completion must be carefully screened and evaluated, since your margin for error will now be reduced nearly to the vanishing point. Along with this will come a necessity for sophistication in both national and world economics, for they will have a significant effect on the fortunes of your enterprise.

Finally, you will discover that your stake in the company will increase enormously, and this will present some new problems of a personal nature.

3

Is Your
Base Camp Secure?

THE process of self-evaluation you are now undergoing should certainly include a careful tally of all your assets. High on the list will be your major accomplishments as a manager—and a definition of how many of them were lucky breaks and how many were the result of your careful craftsmanship. The net result is a plus mark in your ledger in either case, but it is imperative that you do not get in the habit of counting heavily on being favored by the gods in your career progress. The gods are notoriously fickle.

There are several elements to any managerial coup. The first is of course a new and fresh approach to a given problem and its solution. Your proposal will have to be demonstrably better than what has been done before if it is to receive the plaudits of your superiors. They are not about to retire the old model until they are convinced that the substitute is an improvement. So you should cultivate a habit of constructive questioning of every aspect of your job. Adopt and follow the rule that any method you have been using for three years is undeniably obsolete. Someone is always working on a better technique, so why shouldn't you be the one to do it? The first to the wire gets the prize and all the credit.

The second element in engineering a managerial coup is careful, meticulous coordination. Since what you intend to try will entail change, or changes, those concerned have every right to know your plans early in the action. If they are to buy the proposal, they need lead time in planning their activities. The earlier you get them involved, the greater will be their commitment to the project, and the more help you will get from them in pushing it through.

Third, remember the urgency of correct timing all the way down the line. Many fine ideas have been lost, and never even tested, because the environmental conditions were not right at the time. Only your own sensitivity can really help you here. You will have to judge when things are right to make the proposal, when you may expect it to be well received, and when it can actually be put into practice.

There are two timing considerations: fiscal and personnel. Most changes in industry entail considerable money for new equipment, down time in replacing equipment, a learning curve for the new process and getting it up to speed, and perhaps advertising and promotional expenses. Your planning of the costs involved must be impeccable.

Any understatement of them will be fatal to the scheme and to your reputation as an innovator.

You must also consider carefully whether you have enough of the right kind of manpower to make the new idea work. How much retraining will be involved, or will it be necessary to import new blood? Your proposal should include a manning table, with names if possible. Do not be disturbed if changes are made later in this table; if you show the extent to which you have considered every facet involved, you will gain the confidence of your superiors in your plan.

If you have satisfied yourself as to the adequacy of your plan and all its details, the next step is obviously the campaign itself. In terms of his time on the job, the manager is first a teacher and second a salesman. There are few days when he is not immersed in persuading someone to adopt one of his ideas or methods by demonstrating the benefits that will accrue. The same technique must be used by the manager who wants his company to accept his ideas. You wouldn't be where you are unless you had mastered the technique of selling.

As you prepare yourself for the last big jump up in the hierarchy, you should most certainly catalog your accomplishments. This serves two purposes. The first is to help build your self-confidence to the sticking point. You will need as much of it as you can scrape up during the traumatic months ahead. The second is that an inventory of all your accomplishments will help you determine whether you have been missing any bets and whether there are still things in need of improvement which you have neglected too long.

When you get your executive job, you will be dealing

almost exclusively with the new and the different. You will have no time for savoring what has already been done. Your pragmatic leaders will rightly look on your past accomplishments as water under the bridge and will be watching what you are planning for the future. This is good, since it will keep you alert and will add zest to your operation. You must maintain a youthful attitude, but it should be maturely youthful if it is to be functional.

It is important that you get proper credit for your little masterpieces, but your method of accepting credit is also critical to your career. It is nearly certain that others will be involved in any projects you initiate, and you can afford to share the wealth by recognizing their contributions whenever possible. Moreover, your humility should be real. This statement in no way negates the earlier advice to bolster your self-confidence. Humility and recognition of your worth should go hand in hand all the way.

When Was the Last Time You Saved Face for Your Boss?

There is one small part of the managerial job which everyone recognizes, but which is seldom mentioned when managers talk among themselves. That is the fact that once in a while any man will take the rap for his boss. If the boss has painted himself into a corner in such an obvious way that he could become an object of derision to his peers, the subordinate can find real value in publicly accepting the blame. By taking his boss off the hook, at least in public, the subordinate earns several dozen points. The fact that all concerned know the real truth about the matter is

59

immaterial. What counts is saving face for the big man. He will do everything necessary to insure that nothing harmful about the incident enters his subordinate's permanent record, so those who read it later and are not in possession of all the facts will not be misled.

Much more is involved in this kind of situation than your personal feelings or those of your boss. When the leader of a group makes an obvious boner, everyone in the organization feels personally disgraced. Morale is deeply affected, with all the concomitant side effects. Trust and confidence in the group's leadership will be shaken, and the better people will start to look around for a transfer or a job outside the company. If the second-in-command lets it be known that the disaster was his fault, much of this upset can be avoided, even if the real facts are common knowledge. The rest of the crew will actually come out of the affair with more, rather than less, respect for you. The important thing is to keep the public image of the organization untarnished. The mistakes of an underling are never so devastating as those perpetrated by the top man.

You can never be sure that all parties will understand the truth. Some people, including some of your own staff members, may think that you really are as inept as you have allowed yourself to appear. If you enter into the game at all, you are under constraint not to deviate from your role from then on. You must maintain your original position in all subsequent references to the affair. For those who know the real facts, this is of course a recognized part of the game; for those who don't, you are reinforcing a derogatory false impression.

Naturally, the most important factor is that the executives really know the truth of the matter. Their respect for you personally will be enhanced if they realize you are big enough to give this sort of support to your superior. Loyalty to the organization and its leaders is one of the brightest of managerial virtues.

The big question for you is: How often would you be willing to assume this posture? Certainly you do not want to become known as a patsy, willing to accept the blame for an unreasonable number of errors. At this juncture, you must be extremely selective about doing this kind of thing again. No matter how much executives may protest to the contrary, they remain grossly subjective in their methods of selecting new members of their ranks. The policy and procedures may be immensely involved, with checks and balances all over the place, but in the long run, a majority of the new members of the top tier are chosen more through whim than science. We all know that a recent event affects our thinking more strongly than one which occurred months or years ago. If you take the blame for one of your boss's mistakes at just this time, there could be an adverse reaction from those who appoint executives. Although they are apprised of what really happened, they may have doubts about your judgment in putting your head on the block at this particular moment. Your greatest hope during these last months before promotion must be that your superior will not commit any glaring errors.

Finally, we should consider what the biggest man of them all would do. If you had made a mistake, would you be willing to let a subordinate accept public humiliation or would you insist on taking your lumps for your actions? Research has shown that executives are about 58 to 60 percent correct in the decisions they make. This means that none will be free for long from making an error in judgment. If he attempts to bury each mistake in someone else's backyard, the graves will soon become obvious.

These decisions you will have to make for yourself. You alone know how broad your shoulders are, and how much of the boss's load you want to carry for him. There is a fine balance which must be maintained between your interpersonal relationships and the respect of your peers. Smooth and easy interfaces with others are highly desirable; you must have respect to stay in business.

Are You on Target?

In the hurly-burly and excitement of your present campaign for advancement, it could be tragically easy to lose sight of the most important aspect of your promotional possibility. All these moves and countermoves will be vain window dressing unless you keep your present job performance in perfect running order. At your level, your goals and target dates count the most in evaluating the job you do. American industry has become so complex that anyone's final mark will be conditioned to a large extent by the inputs he receives from others. Missing deadlines would be seriously detrimental not only to your own performance, but to that of many other managers.

The basis for successful management in maintaining deadlines is planning. For every principal component of your work output, you must have several alternative plans for arriving at your goals. For example, if your main function is manufacturing, you should keep in constant touch with procurement, to be sure there will be no shortages of critical raw materials. Secondary and tertiary vendors must be kept on tap at all times, to insure a smooth flow of necessary components. If you are in finance, maintaining an open connection with several sources of lines of credit is of paramount importance. It is for this reason that most large companies have accounts with several banks. If your area of responsibility is engineering, you must stay on top of every facet of your technology, so that external changes or the emergence of new techniques and materials will not outdate your expertise overnight.

The twin to planning in insuring that you meet your deadlines is, of course, control. The chances are that by now your operations are complex enough to require a tool such as PERT/time or its equivalent. Remember that monitoring this kind of complicated control is more than a one-man job. You must make some nicely calculated delegations to members of your staff to insure successful attainment of your time goals. You should be the coordinator, rather than the laborer, in this activity.

It is in this aspect of your job that some of the most fruitful areas for delegation lie. By passing to your subordinates much of the responsibility for insuring that deadlines are met, you will achieve some particularly effective training and development. Your people can increase their understanding of your total area of responsibility; they can grow in personal stature and knowledge; and they can make huge gains in the self-confidence so necessary for good managerial performance. In addition, the development of a smoothly functioning team effort leads to esprit de corps, with all the benefits it can give an organization.

None of these things can be done in a vacuum. Your need for adequate communication will never be greater. Your people must know what is required of them; your peers must be brought into the arena; and most certainly your superiors must be kept informed. At the same time, you will have to balance what you require from others with what will be required from you. This is the give-and-take of management. For whatever you expect from your peers, you will owe something in return. The balancing of managerial books will allow for not one penny's variance between credits and debits in the ledger. It is hardly necessary to point out that you must employ the same sort of meticulous planning and controlling to keep yourself even with your peers and that, for every iota of cooperation you expect to receive from them, one will be exacted from you.

While all this is going on routinely, another constraint will be laid upon you which can be more onerous than any of the rest. At all times, you must be aware of external conditions which can have an effect on what you are doing. On any given date, you may be required to go into feverish activity to compensate for independent variables on the outside over which you have no measure of control. Your target dates, and those of your peers, are all subject to renegotiation up to the last minute. This is the point at which your alternative planning will prove its worth and can act as a lifesaver. It is the ace in the hole that can keep you in the game, when it seems that the cards are stacked against you.

If you have started to feel a noticeable upturn in your anxiety level, now is perhaps the time to reinforce one of our major tenets: The higher the stakes, the greater your involvement must be, and the greater the effort required of you if you are to have a chance of winning. Alertness is the sharpest arrow you can have in your quiver during this part of your career development, and its companion is sensitivity to the probable reactions of others to the conditions of the contest. You must not only meet your goals and deadlines, but must do so in a manner acceptable to your fellow workers at all levels. You will reach full maturity as a manager only when you are expert in weaving all these elements into an acceptable product for your public, which includes your fellow workers as well as your customers. Stature in management is a mosaic, reflecting many colorations, components, reactions, feelings, and outcomes.

Now, relax. We have been putting the pressure on you in several areas. Do the arithmetic, do the planning, do the controlling we have specified, and then fall back and regroup. The rest is in the lap of the gods. You are, after all, a human being, and you have a right to recoup the energy you have so far had to expend. Perhaps you should now take a weekend off and forget the whole damned thing.

How Many Former Subordinates Are Now Your Peers?

As finesse in management increases, the manager is measured more and more on his ability to develop his subordinates. There was a time when the supervisor felt jealous of, and threatened by, any of his subordinates who showed much promise. He feared that he might be unseated by the comers if he recognized their potential. Remnants of this attitude exist in some of the more backward managers, but on the whole it has been replaced by the realization that we are going to need many more managers and that there will be room to spare on the rungs of the ladder for all the good ones. Therefore, a recognized part of the supervisor's job must be the careful nurturing of any managerial talent he discovers among his people. (Remember that no one ever "develops" anyone else; all development is self-development. But the supervisor does provide the climate in which development takes place, and he can make that climate good or bad.)

Every supervisor who has entered management from your group is another star in your crown as a leader. Many organizational development groups keep meticulous records in this area; some even go so far as to weight various factors in the promotional history, such as the openness of lines of progression and the availability of opportunities for entry into supervision. Thus it is natural that the success of your protégés downstream after promotion be recorded. And with each entry in the record you will accumulate credits as a manager both for the numbers of your employees who have been promoted and for their success as supervisors once they are there.

Your cultivation of your people is one indication of your professionalism. Doctors and lawyers take great delight in "discovering" likely candidates for entry into their fields. It would be helpful if the field of management had professional preparatory schools comparable to our schools of medicine and law. There are none—yet. But who is to say when management will have accrued enough professionalism to enable such schools to open, with a concomitant shift toward licensing of managerial candidates? Earning a degree in management, and gaining a certificate or license to practice management, would not guarantee success any more than an M.D. degree plus an internship automatically guarantees success in the practice of medicine. But such an educational and licensing procedure would be progress toward a desirable and needed upgrading of the jobs of those who run our businesses and industries.

The pressures on you to help insure a succession of qualified managers will increase rather than slacken in the years to come. There is as yet no visible sign that limits should be placed on the numbers of properly prepared men and women who enter management. To date, we have not had the courage to face all the ramifications of the current shortage of managers.

This challenge to you is many faceted. First, and of primary importance, is your ability to sense potential. This is analogous to the ability of a diamond cutter to visualize his final product as he studies his uncut gem.

Second, you must have the patience and the ingenuity to attract the attention, interest, and motivation of your candidate. His promise is well hidden, and he may not be conscious of any desire to become a leader. Third, if you do become the mentor of a candidate for management, you must carefully nurture the raw talent, act as a catalyst to help it grow and acquire a polish capable of attracting the attention of those responsible for supervisory selection. Fourth and finally, you will owe your candidate loyalty and support as he makes the adjustment to his first supervisory position. He would never forgive you if you abandoned him at that most crucial time.

If you have a green thumb in the managerial garden, make the most of it, both for the sake of your profession as a whole and for purely selfish reasons. It is money in your personal career bank to receive the credit for helping many of your people up the ladder. Moreover, your protégés will surely show their loyalty to you for having given them a hand. It never hurts to have friends in strategic places when you face troubles of your own. It goes without saying that you will vitiate this advantage if you play the part of a Shylock calling a loan, no matter what the circumstances; but such action will not be necessary if you have been correct in your evaluation of those you have helped. They will respond of their own accord when your need is evident.

In the last analysis, your greatest reward will be a quiet, personal, inward, and ongoing satisfaction at the success of those you once led. Actually, in all probability they will still think of you as one of their leaders.

Can You Trust Your People?
Can They Trust You?

In the managerial literature, and in conversations among management people, many platitudes and many clichés are overworked on the subject of trust and confidence between superior and subordinate. It is fine and honorable to assume the personal integrity of every member of management, but the statistical probability is that the presence of this characteristic will vary widely in such a large population. Certainly, the great majority of managers are honest and are capable of giving and receiving trust. American business, and the country along with it, would come to a crashing halt if this were not so. But we would be less than realistic if we were to deny that once in a while we run afoul of a member of management whose honesty is open to question. It is for these rare cases that we must be alert.

It may sound paradoxical (perhaps even immoral) to suggest that there are *degrees* of honesty. Our grandfathers would have been outraged at such a concept. Our fathers would have reacted a trifle less strongly, and we as realists must face the fact that there are degrees of dishonesty. The most blatant type—and the one evoked in most people's minds at the mention of dishonesty—is fiscal. No one is willing to trust a man who is incapable of distinguishing between his material belongings and those of others. Such a person is given short shrift until he redeems himself and proves incontrovertibly that he has reformed. But the area of intellectual dishonesty is another matter entirely. Here the black and the white are badly smudged into gray field. What is grossly wrong in one man's view is completely defensible in another's.

One of the special forms of honesty of most concern to the manager is personal loyalty. How much fealty do you owe your supervisor, and how much is due you from your subordinates? What kind of situation triggered by an action of your superior would cause you to turn it to your advantage? Under what circumstances would you expect your boss to go to bat for you? These ethico-philosophical questions are of great importance to your mental health throughout your managerial career. Most certainly, you can expect no more from your people than you are willing to give them—and maybe just a shade less, since yours is the greater responsibility.

It is hard to imagine being willing to work with a staff member whom you found impossible to trust, yet such situations exist. You might face up to balancing a priceless talent of his against the fact that you would have to watch his every step. His contribution to your organization might

69

be of so high a caliber that you would be willing to take the calculated risk of his being after your scalp. You might be self-confident enough to think you could outwit him at the crucial moment. Remember, you are now at a hierarchical altitude where the gold glitters, but the air is thin. Just what is your vital capacity? Is his boost with one hand greater than his drag with the other? Necessary decisions of this sort add a kind of piquancy to your life.

Your actions in this arena will have to be governed by your own special and personal code of ethics. The only person in business you will have to live with for the rest of your life is yourself; nowhere else is the Golden Rule more applicable than in your daily work. You must extend the kind of trust and good treatment that you hope to receive from your associates. Without this as a basis, you are totally lost.

Think twice before you dismiss this issue as inconsequential. It is one of the basic determinants of the quality of your interactions with everyone around you; it will set the tone of your professional reputation. Lack of trust in others is one of the most easily discernible traits any person can show. If you are defensive, you will evoke defensive responses, and all contacts will be conducted under an insupportable strain.

Another warning should be carefully heeded. Many a fine manager has suffered severely from the shock of a trusted lieutenant's defection. The shock is difficult to recover from. If your own character and reputation are what they should be, your chances of surviving such a betrayal are extremely high; your peers are men of perception, and they are perfectly capable of drawing the obvious conclusions from the facts. The last thing you need is to suffer from a backlash which might damage your effectiveness. Your attitude should be: no revenge! His peer group will mete out punishment in its own way much more effectively than you could single-handedly.

The strong can trust; the weak must fear. If you have done your job in selecting, coaching, and developing your staff, you have little to fear from them in the normal course of events. This statement is made in full realization of the higher stakes for which you are now playing and the greater abilities and deeper drives of those who are working for you. Seldom could the acts of one of your subordinates be definitive in determining your course. What is important is the sum of the acts and attitudes of all those who are working for you; this total will be under the scrutiny of those who govern your future. Be honest yourself, expect honesty from others, and sleep well at night.

Are You Really an Old Pro?

At this point it would be wise to examine one of the assumptions under which we have been working so far: that you are an old pro as a manager. Proficiency in the management field is the product of so many variables that it is difficult to analyze. And good operation at one level of management requires skills quite different from those demanded of you when you move up, echelon by echelon. As a first-line supervisor, your major (and critical) functions were those of relating to your people, explaining and implementing company policy, and getting the product out the door. Your upward communications were limited mainly to progress reports and reports of controls. When

71

you became a middle manager, you shifted gears; you now are managing managers, and your operation has been modified because of their different mental set and (usually) greater personal motivation and identification with the enterprise. For the first time, you are now required to use your powers of conceptualization on the job, although not nearly as much as you will when you become an executive.

In middle management, your expertise is often measured by your ability to coordinate and to compromise. You are the catalyst for the melding of many diverse elements into a viable whole, and you must keep track of several different functions and activities. Since your sphere of influence has been widened many times, you have begun to have meaningful personal associations with many other members of management, both inside and outside your business. It was disturbing at first to find that your relationships with others are both deeper and more superficial than they were when you were on the first line. They are deeper because you go into greater depth in your business associations; they are superficial because your contacts with some of your associates are much more infrequent than those you had with the smaller group of peers. By this time you have probably adjusted to the fact that your contacts with your executive boss are less directive than they were when you reported to a middle manager. You are more on your own than you were when you entered supervision.

These new, or changed, factors of evaluation of your work confused you at first. You may even now have a residual feeling of frustration when you think of how your superior measures your efficiency, since so many of the working elements of your job are not quantifiable in any real sense. Of course, you may be operating under a well-designed system of management by objectives, or you may be required to present semiannual performance standards to be negotiated with your boss. But you and he both know that these are not the whole story of how you are doing. There will always be some subjective segments to the total assessment of your performance, and their aggregate seems more gross as you rise on the ladder.

From here on out, the most critical measurement of your performance will be the one you make on yourself. This is so because of the greater degree of self-determination under which you are now operating, and this facet will again increase when you become an executive. Thus your personal standards of performance are much more important now and will continue to become more critical to your success. For the most part, you will have to develop and standardize your own bench marks, rather than depend on your superior for this signal. Naturally, he will still have some strong opinions on this subject, but your operation will be dependent upon your creative efforts at setting standards for yourself. You will be much closer to your work than will your boss, or anyone else, because of the large measure of self-direction and autonomy you now enjoy.

Directly in line with subjectivity of measurement, another consideration about your present and future work must not be forgotten: your increasing professionalism. Actually, it will loom larger as you go on to finish your business career. There is more to professionalism than your growth and development as an individual. Your environment will demand more and more professionalism of you as time goes on. An irreversible trend is clearly apparent in the business community: We are being forced to professionalism as the business world becomes more complex day by day. We see interrelationships and interdependencies proliferating almost as we watch. Liaison and coordination activities are taking more of your time, and will continue to do so. Some managers mourn the fact that it has become well nigh impossible to operate any more as an entrepreneur, with all the attendant heady feelings of power and accomplishment. Nevertheless, the facts of life are incontrovertible; we shall have to adjust to them if we value our personal success. Since we can't lick them, we might as well join them.

*   *   *

This chapter has asked you to catalog your achievements to date. In point of fact, the only ones that will count heavily in your chances for advancement are the recent ones. But it is still a good exercise to review your big personal successes, if for no other reason than to bolster your self-confidence and give you renewed courage. You have often saved face for your boss in the past; now you must decide whether—and when—you would want to do so again.

Your current job performance must be topnotch; it is being scrutinized daily by those who make decisions about promotions. One major measurement will be the numbers of your former employees who have been promoted into management. Individually and collectively, they make fine ornaments in your managerial headdress. You should also review the depth of the mutual trust between you and your people. Finally, *are* you an old pro?

4

What Makes You
Think You're Different?

ALL progress is the result of deviations from the established ways of doing things. In modern society, most changes are deliberately instituted by the group leader and then reinforced by his group. Despite this fact, extremely strong pressures are put on all members of management at all levels to stick closely to some rigidly prescribed norms. In most enterprises, behavioral patterns are clearly delineated, and the rewards for conformity and the punishments for deviation are firmly established. As an executive, you will be expected to conform closely to the rules. You must never, under any circumstances, get a reputation for trying to effect drastic changes overnight.

Leaders, however, are usually inner-directed and generally less subject to group pressures than are people who are followers by nature. Thus many men who reach the executive level have a history of failure to comply with established norms. Each of these men at various points in his career came to the rational decision that a particular norm was unrealistic or ineffective, and thus subject to replacement by another norm he thought would be more functional. He was ready to face censure by the group in order to make a run at changes in the organization.

If you wish to become an executive, you must be willing to accept change as a way of life. To prepare yourself for that important aspect of the executive's role, your self-development program should include an examination of the ways in which you differ from your subordinates, your boss, and your peers. As part of that examination, you must determine which of your characteristics are innate and which you have deliberately grafted onto your personality. You should also consider the possibility of eradicating any inherent characteristics which you find to be abrasive and dysfunctional in the business world. We are speaking as if your personality, early in middle age, were still a plastic thing. It is. No manager or executive dare set in concrete any of his personality traits (as differentiated from qualities of character) at any time during his business life. Both internal and external factors are subject to too many changes for you to remain rigid. Many managers have great difficulty in maintaining this high degree of personal flexibility. Because they possess notable strengths, they may tend to do a little steamrolling. This technique may flatten resistance, but it will also make the managers less effective crew members.

How Do You Differ from Your Subordinates?

Because organizational development will become increasingly important to you when you become an executive, there is no better place to begin the activity than with your present organization. You should identify as completely as possible the differences between yourself and your people and estimate their effect on the total efforts of your group. How many of these differences were the products of chance, and how many did you deliberately introduce? How would you characterize their sum as a vector in your group's effectiveness? What actions should you now take to correct any uncomfortable interpersonal relationships growing out of these differences? Are communications among your staff members, and between you and them, suffering because of these variations in personality?

This matter of being different will obviously contribute to the sense of isolation that will characterize your executive life. You will have to get used to the fact that the people who empathize with your mental outlook will be leaders rather than followers. The latter find it more comfortable to go along with things as they are rather than to question their merit or efficiency.

Any man who wishes to rise to the top of his group must have not only a fine intuition about what alterations are needed or desirable, but also the influence and expertise to bring his group along with him. He must be sensitive to the delicate timing essential for acceptance of change by his people. His patience will be tried, but he must force himself to wait for the group to catch up with him in conceptualizing and accepting the changes he initiates. We all know impetuous leaders who have been successful, but they are a minority.

Your career as an executive will be a series of mileposts indicating the changes you effectuate. If you are a wise leader, you will assign priorities to the changes you deem desirable and be willing to forgo some of them so that the more important ones can be realized.

Your personal idiosyncrasies will of necessity put a stamp of individuality on your working group. They are purely a function of the way you express your leadership. Your characteristics will be a governing factor in the staff you gather, because they will either attract or repel others. There will be a modicum of trial and error in getting together a permanent group, since it is not always possible to predict how anyone will react to your leadership. As one of your developmental activities, you could benefit from taking a series of seminars in the use of the managerial grid. This combination of modified sensitivity training and experimentation with various managerial styles can be most illuminating. Because these experiments will be carried out away from your regular work group, none of the mistakes you make will affect your people.

If you choose your staff members partly on the basis of their differences from one another, friction will sometimes arise. Some direct confrontations about issues is healthy, as long as all concerned are careful to keep personalities out of the picture. Of course, this is not always possible, and when disagreements arise you will have to play it by ear to keep estrangements at a minimum. Any irreconcilable differences which arise at this level in the hierarchy can haunt the people involved for the rest of their careers in the company.

In forming your organization, you will be subjected to the great temptation of indulging in a cult of personality. It is easy to exaggerate the need for originality of thought and action from you and from your people. Most certainly, the ability to motivate is needed, but like any other characteristic, it must not become a vice. A collection of prima donnas can never be welded into a functional team, and in the last analysis it is your team that will win or lose the battle.

How Do You Differ from Your Boss?

The leader who surrounds himself with people too much like himself is increasing the possibility of failure by concentrating common faults or too uniform a point of view. At the middle management or executive level, it is mandatory that all sides of every question be thoroughly examined before any decisions are made; modern business is overwhelmingly a team effort. For this reason, members of the management team are often chosen on the basis of their differences from, rather than their similarities to, the leader. Your boss may have brought you into middle management so that your strengths could compensate for his weaknesses in particular areas. Perhaps he noticed that you did superior planning or that your relationships with employees were noticeably better than were those of others in his sphere of influence.

In your attempt to draw a continuing self-portrait, you

should list and document the major differences between yourself and your boss in mental and physical traits as well as in operating methods. Then decide whether these differences constitute strengths or weaknesses in yourself. This exercise will give you more inputs for your self-development program. Most certainly you should counsel with your superior during this process.

Another aspect of this self-study should be an effort to learn from your boss's strengths. You can afford to spend considerable time examining his methods of operation to see what has made him successful or what is keeping him from higher achievement. This activity could be beneficial for both you and your supervisor. If your reasoned conclusion is that his performance would improve if he modified some of his methods, it is your duty to communicate your belief to him. This is one facet of the process of delegating upward which you have been practicing for some time. Of course, the delicate touch is required here, but he will probably be grateful for your comments if they open his eyes to a weak spot in his method of operation.

Can You See over the Heads of All Your Peers?

Your self-evaluation would be incomplete without a look at the competition—your peers. In what significant ways are you different from the majority of them? How much, and how often, does your thinking differ from theirs? Is there a history of friction between you because of these differences, or have you been able to reconcile them and maintain smooth relationships?

In one or more major categories you must be better

than any other single member of middle management who might be in the running for an executive job. At this level, everyone realizes there is no time left for favoritism. Of course, in family-held concerns the crown normally passes to a member of the family, but in public corporations those concerned feel more responsible to the stockholders and are more intent on providing the best possible management for the enterprise. This makes sense from several standpoints, not the least of which is the preservation of the organization as a whole. Competition being what it is, the best-managed business firms have enough trouble maintaining their relative positions without taking the risk of elevating the wrong man to a position of real authority. Too much is at stake.

So your job is to compare your qualifications with those of others who are in the running so as to ascertain whether there is anything you should do immediately to better your competitive position in the race.

It should be said here that your developmental procedure will begin to change, to become less formal and much more personal. A good deal of your growth will be the result of your one-to-one interactions with your peers, most of whom will be outside your own enterprise. It is essential that you get as broad a perspective as possible on all your problem areas. You have no time for tunnel vision. But you can hardly be expected to be objective enough about yourself to make this self-evaluation without help. Go to the pros. Call upon the professional students of organization within your company, or enlist the services of a management consultant in compiling the relevant data. Your objective is well-rounded development—including, as we said earlier, some expertise in economics. The total point score will win the prize; you will have to be high on the totem pole in all significant marks, although it may not be necessary for you to be the top man in any single category.

To do this part of your developmental job well, you will have to keep some records. Your files should contain a carefully documented analysis of good performance in any area by any of your peers. This analysis should include a step-by-step narrative of what took place, comments on why the action was effective, and notes as to ways in which you would have conducted the action to make it better. This may be a second-guessing device, but it is effective in giving you data on good procedures.

It would also be useful to perform the same sort of post-mortem on any failure of your peers. Was it caused by the leader's deficiencies in technical, human, or conceptual skills? Did the failure result from a breakdown in communication at a crucial point, or were controls dysfunctional or lacking? Was the leader unable to sell the project to his people enough to get their wholehearted commitment? Did he fail to get across the urgent need for this action, and were the objectives a little hazy in the minds of those who were doing the actual work?

All these questions are germane. Your breakdown of these and other factors can be quite instructive. You can learn from the failures of others as well as from your own, but to do so takes a special mental set and particularly good observational and analytical procedures.

In measuring the stature of your peers, you should be equally concerned about the performance of their groups. In fact, the best method of entry is often through a look at the group rather than at its leadership. A reflection of the manager's actions could be more instructive than a direct look, which would be subject to the bias of your personal feelings toward him, friendly or otherwise.

You are now in the throes of what may be your first efforts at organizational analysis on a personal basis. This will become an important tool to you as you advance into the actual executive position. The health of any organization requires that such analysis be done on a continuing basis. Groups of people at work must be examined at regular intervals, just as the individual members must take an annual physical as a precautionary measure. Most assuredly, we do not quantify human behavior, nor can it be fitted to any mathematical formula with absolute values assigned to performance in any area or facet of the job. But we can, by astute observation and the application of our best efforts at analysis, come close to a rank order of managerial performance which will be valid and reliable.

It is to be hoped that the way you rank your peers will not be too far from the executives' estimate of them, or you may be in for a serious disappointment. Of course, your objectives are different, but that does not alter the effectiveness of the technique for helping you to better your position, since you will put to good use the things you learn from your exercise. That is why it is of the utmost urgency that you start this analysis early in your campaign for the executive's chair. After discovering your deficiencies, you have to allow time enough to rectify them, and such things are not accomplished overnight. However, your increments of time in campaigning for an executive position are measured in years rather than months. You cannot expect immediate or spectacular success within months of setting your sights on the highest rung on the ladder.

How Tough Are You Physically?

The demands made on your body by your job are greater now than they will be when you become an executive, simply because you now interact with many more people each day than you will in the top echelon. Moreover, as the head man, you will have more discretionary time and will be able to exercise more control over the allocation of your working hours. Right now, you are being driven so hard by the demands of your people, your peers, and your superiors that there is hardly a moment of the day you can call your own. Moreover, you often find it necessary to take work home at night, or over the weekend, to get your own job completed.

All this has been a severe test of your physical toughness and stamina ever since you became a member of management. Most of the time you feel as if you are chained to your desk, and your lack of sufficient physical activity has had its effect. You would probably prefer not to be reminded of how much weight you have gained as a middle manager. Your golf score is soaring because you don't find the time to get out on the course regularly. Homework has eroded the time you used to spend in little maintenance chores around the house.

You have no doubt taken advantage of your company's offer of free annual physical examinations. You have shucked off the doctor's warnings about the sedentary habits you have acquired on your job. Your life will become even more sedentary when you become an executive. Although you will have a measure of control over the distribution of your time, the demands upon it will be there, inescapably. The years ahead will be the ultimate test of your physical strength. Success as an executive is closely associated with your ability to call upon your physical resources at all times, with no time for illness.

The only reasonable answer to this problem is to enter upon a planned program of physical toning and weight control. Many executives join a health club or take organized and regular gymnasium exercise. Maybe you should now start to make some of your business dates on the golf course, however good or poor your game. Because of the undeniably close correlation between the mental strain of your job and your physical well-being, a planned and executed exercise period during the day will do much to relieve mental stress. Check your doctor about the best method to use.

To keep a sane and reasonable balance between your physical inactivity on the job and the exercise required to continue being a normally functioning middle-aged man, you must maintain sane attitudes both toward life in general and toward your job. The basis of this attitude is your refusal to panic under pressure, with the resultant sacrifice of your health. You will find it necessary to face each problem calmly, without allowing pressure to build up. If you can do this, you will have set the proper climate for problem solving. You already have the other necessary techniques.

Resilience and the ability to recover from attack are your goals, and always should be. You should expect to get tired—even exhausted—after a long hard session, but you must also be able to recover your stride and your strength quickly. You will not be allowed the luxury of a long recuperation after an intensive struggle with people or things. If they knock you through the ropes, you must be able to shake your head, climb back into the arena, and be ready to go again.

We must counter this with a reminder that it is always foolhardy to ignore symptoms of physical malfunction. Get your physician into the act quickly, and let him take over. But there is no point in consulting him if you ignore his advice afterward. He will be sympathetic and understanding about your job demands, but his primary responsibility is your physical well-being.

As you succeed in improving your physical condition, you will find new zest and pleasure in your job. As your stamina increases through exercise and diet, your capacity for work, your endurance, and your decision-making ability will all increase, with noticeable overall improvement in your job performance. Your physical and mental health are so closely intermeshed as to be inseparable; taking care of yourself is one chore you can't delegate.

How Tough Are You Mentally?

Although there have been highly successful top men who fought bad health all their lives, the records are bare of cases of executives who lacked mental resilience. You must be capable of taking all attacks thrown at you without suffering mental shock. You cannot afford to be thrown off balance.

Mental toughness should never be confused with an attitude of distrust of those around you. The higher you are on the company ladder, the more you will be forced to trust others. If you suspect everyone of ulterior motives, they will develop the same attitude toward you. You will demonstrate your mental toughness if you can maintain that general posture of trust but recover immediately from the effects of discovering that a particular person cannot be trusted. Mental toughness is not exhibited by the man who tries to bully his way through opposition to attain his goals. Your position and personal qualifications give you more power than most people with whom you come in contact. It is eminently unfair to use this power indiscriminately.

The most glaring danger of forcing your will on others at all times is that you have a chance of being wrong. Unless you stop to listen to your critics, you can lay no claim to mental toughness. The man who is mentally tough does not brag or build up his ego at the expense of others. To do so is one of the surer signs of personal insecurity and an attempt to compensate for it.

Mental toughness is basically characterized by a continuing and objective questioning of all data the executive must process personally. Although he can afford to trust those he has picked to work with him, he need not accept any of their inputs without asking for documentation. Most of all, he must examine his own mental processes. What makes us think that our decisions are necessarily valid unless we have checked and rechecked every step of our way to the decision? One of the major indicators of mental toughness is the ability to bounce back from defeat and attack the same problem again. History is full of the successes of great men who refused to admit they could be beaten. They were concerned with winning the war rather than the battle.

It is difficult for a person innately sensitive to criticism to develop mental toughness, but it can be done. Since in this case you are working in the area of emotions, the road will be longer and a little rockier, but that is no reason to abandon the effort. This is another aspect of your self-discipline, and one that will demand a lot of attention, since it is easily observed by your associates. The man who lacks this trait leaves himself especially vulnerable if he tries to function as an executive.

One of the most useful, and yet dangerous, attributes of the mentally tough person is his ability to remain steadfast under criticism. No executive can afford to be afraid of going it alone if he thinks the situation calls for it. One of the assumptions made about you when you were picked to become a middle manager was that you would have the strength of your convictions sufficient to carry you through. Your enterprise will probably show little or no progress unless you are willing to make and abide by decisions that will be unpopular. In fact, your final success as a manager will be measured in exactly these situations. Of course, to exhibit mental toughness in this way is dangerous if you come to a wrong decision and push it through.

Your mental toughness will be the basis for all the real respect your peers and your subordinates have for you. Since you are the nominal leader of at least one major segment of the business, they will demand that you accept the responsibilities of your job and keep trying to meet the goals of your organization with all that is in you. Most certainly, at this time you should be thinking a great deal about all the implications of the job you are seeking. You must fit them all into your concept of the position of an executive and be prepared to discharge each of these burdens as it is laid upon you. You will have few people to turn to for help once you are there. Instead, you will constantly be called upon to help others.

One last point about mental toughness: There is no place in it for personal bitterness on any subject; bitterness usually has its basis in self-pity, and the executive has no time for that personal luxury. He can only assume that whatever milk has been spilled was sour anyway.

To recapitulate: Mental toughness is one of the requirements for success as an executive. You *must* have it. It can be cultivated and developed, like all the other desirable attributes of the job. Since it is largely a matter of personal attitude, you have final control over its development, and little help is available from others in achieving this personal objective. It must become an integral part of your business life. At the same time, you must be careful that this one trait does no gratuitous injury to those around you. This is the area in which you will have to maintain constant alertness. You will treat yourself more harshly than you will treat most of those working for you.

What Was Your Last Big Mistake?

For the record, and for balance in your self-analysis, you should review the errors in your middle management career that gave you the greatest problems. No manager can live without making mistakes, but you should always learn from them and take care not to repeat them. Any normal human being has great difficulty in being objective about his own bad performance. It is easy to excuse ourselves and to rationalize our actions. You must successfully fight this impulse and take a cold, hard look at the entire situation. What elements led you into a trap? Were they circumstances having to do with people or with things? Did you receive bad advice from a peer or your supervisor? Did you make decisions on the basis of insufficient data? Most embarrassing of all, was the error caused by purely faulty reasoning on your part?

If you are to put your errors into perspective and profit from them, it is essential that you get the real answers to these and other germane questions.

Further research could be beneficial, especially a few months or a year after the occurrence. What were the long-range results? How much money was involved? Were any other people seriously affected by your course of action? The ripples from a single stone dropped in the pool often cover a wide area. Of course, you must not allow this process to make you despondent or defensive. The purpose is purely constructive, as the results of your examination should be.

Seldom is it necessary to draw the attention of anyone else to this study of your errors. In the course of your performance reviews with your boss, he may recall them as a matter of record, but if the relationship between you is solid, he will not dwell on them. Even in listing them at all, he should be concerned with whatever positive value could be distilled from them.

As a supervisor of other managers, you must maintain the kind of attitude toward their instances of bad judgment as you would want your boss to exhibit toward yours. This is especially difficult to do, since their performance naturally reflects directly upon yours, and we could defend the thesis that the sum of their actions equals the total of your work production. It would be easy for you to become highly critical of an error by one of your people, but in the long run there is nothing to be gained from this reaction.

As to your peers, you have nothing to excuse yourself for to them, unless one of them was hurt by an action of yours. Naturally, they have also had their bad moments, and there is nothing to be gained from developing an atmosphere of recrimination. It is bad for all concerned and is totally indefensible. Only one group of people have you completely at their mercy if they are involved: your customers. If an error of yours has hurt them, you cannot avoid explaining thoroughly what happened in an attempt to make restitution.

Finally, you must condition yourself to keep a positive outlook toward all aspects of your work at all times. It is the only way you can hope for continuing success in your job as a manager and as an executive.

*　　*　　*

This chapter has examined the question of whether you are really different from other managers. The answer to this is always a categorical yes. Each of us is unique, so of course we differ from one another. The question then is: In what ways should you be different if you hope to succeed as an executive? One of the more obvious answers is that you should be inventive and innovative. Living as you do in a society of constant change, your business will always be in a state of flux; as an executive, you will have to guide and manage those changes.

It is important that you catalog for yourself the ways in which you are different from your boss. Are you strong in his areas of weakness, or perhaps less than a titan in his areas of strength? Were you chosen to be a middle manager largely to offset his weaknesses? These are important points to consider in evaluating your chances for promotion to the executive echelon. This survey should provide. some important new entries in your personal development program and should be followed by some positive action.

At this point you must also take a hard look at the way you stack up against all your peers. Every one of them must be considered a possible rival for promotion. Once again, you will make notations, with action to follow.

It is of primary importance that you cultivate and develop both physical and mental toughness, in order to meet the greater demands that will be placed on you. Remember that toughness means resilience, the ability to rebound from a blow without being bent out of shape. For all intents and purposes, toughness is an attitude of mind.

In looking at your qualities of difference, you should examine the errors you have made since you became a manager, but only for the purpose of learning from them.

All these new and difficult steps in your continuing self-development program may discourage you, but if you should throw in the towel now, the executive echelon would conclude that you had failed one of the definitive tests given to all candidates for promotion. To avoid this judgment, you will have to undertake as rigorous a training effort as any athlete if you are to be promoted again and if you are to be a success in your higher position.

5

Do You Like
Being the Target for Today?

HAVE you ever been shot at from ambush? Any member of the armed forces, present or past, who has seen action could probably answer this question in the affirmative. In your position as a middle manager you may already have experienced the extreme discomfort of being the target of an ambush. But the frequency of such occurrences and the accuracy of the marksmanship will increase noticeably when you reach the executive level. At that position of eminence in the hierarchy, snipers will automatically aim at you.

It is unnerving to discover that people you hardly know feel animosity toward you. It is one thing to be under attack from someone out in the open; it is a different thing entirely to have missiles coming your way which have been fired by unidentified assailants. Your first and logical reaction might be to ignore these attacks because they have no basis in truth. Unfortunately, this technique does not work. As an executive, you will be a public figure, at least for the people who constitute your enterprise. Public figures can be effective only when their reputations are above reproach, and you must not allow yourself to become the victim of character assassination.

It is for this reason that you will be forced to organize a communications ring, one of whose principal functions will be to trace and destroy rumors inimical to you. Moreover, this must be done quickly and effectively if you are to protect yourself. The group need not be large, but its members must be chosen for their personal loyalty to you, their alertness, and their sensitivity, and they must be strategically placed. In this situation, there is no need for routine or periodic reporting; your communicators will swing into action only in the event of an attack upon you. That is when you must waste no time in taking countermeasures.

The most (and really the only) effective step is to make certain that you have correctly identified the people active in disseminating the rumors. The method for fighting them will have to vary according to your estimation of their strengths and weaknesses. In some cases, you might choose open and direct confrontation; in other situations, you might decide that a roundabout counteroffensive would be more effective. Your tactics will vary according to the time lapse between initiation of the attack and your discovery of its sources. If you are lucky enough to come upon it early, that fact may be sufficient to kill the rumor. If a noticeable time should elapse, you might have to organize a therapeutic counteroffensive.

The methods your anonymous enemies use will be maddeningly hard to pin down and fight against. Slight distortions of the truth, or the omission of a pertinent fact, can totally distort the image you present to your public. You will know that you have really arrived at executive stature when jokes about you begin to circulate. As we all know, many a politician has been laughed out of office. And you must face the fact that your new position has many political elements to it.

It would be easy to develop a false sense of security by reassuring yourself and everybody around you that the people who really count will not be taken in by specious statements or false rumors. Unfortunately, however, it is easy to listen to canards about our leaders. Although your associates might not be easily persuaded that any accusations made against you are true, they could still harbor a half-belief that could be terribly damaging to your leadership position.

It is both easy and hard to guard your personal organization against this sort of Trojan Horse infiltration. Your associates have much more personal knowledge of your probity than strangers could possibly have, and they would find it hard to believe something of you which they know to be completely foreign to your nature. But they may be reticent about coming to you with any rumors they hear lest such an act imply a certain disloyalty. So they are likely to fret about the possibility that there is truth in a hearsay item rather than approach you to get immediate clarification and negation.

Today's youth have the best advice for you in this situation: Keep your cool. Never could a panicky reaction be more devastating than in this fix. Your decisions and actions must be made quickly, but they must be carefully calculated and based on the most rigorous thought and analysis. Most important of all, you must be able to present documentation for whatever statements you make in rebuttal; obviously, your enemies cannot be similarly prepared, since their accusations are not founded in truth.

You must recognize that you will be the subject of rumor from here on out—in both your business and your personal life. You will never again be able to separate the two into nice little compartments; this is another penalty for becoming a public figure. Never before have you been required to exercise emotional maturity as unremittingly as you will when you become an executive. We might even go so far as to say that you must become detached from personalities—your own included—for the rest of your business life. Learn to channel your emotions into other areas. Concentration on your family and outside friends can provide great compensation.

What's Your Reaction Time?

Related to the intensity of your feelings when you are attacked from ambush is the speed of your reaction. Essentially, that speed is what makes the difference between Sunday drivers and professional racers. The champion of any contest is the one whose nerves and muscles respond a millisecond faster than those of his competitors. You face countless emergency situations in your business life, and in each case the survival of your career depends on how quickly you respond to the first signals of trouble. The most intricate and beautifully conceptualized planning in the world is useless if you put it into effect too late. In these days, controls after the fact are rapidly approaching extinction, since they are no longer effective in protecting the manager. The directing function you employ with your subordinates must provide sufficient lead time for them to put your plans into action. You have become accustomed to this way of working ever since you first became a supervisor, but the numbers and kinds of situations demanding extremely short reaction time will multiply when you become an executive.

In its simplest terms, quick reaction is closely akin to intuition. You can probably recall occasions when you started to act almost before you were conscious of a need to do so. Later, on reflection, you may have found it impossible to determine what actually triggered your action. You were sure only that a particular action, or series of actions, was called for.

You might infer from this that speed of reaction is useful to you only when your business safety is threatened. This is not so. Many of your coups and triumphs, many of your giant steps forward, will be possible only if you react quickly enough to beat your competitors. You are now at that time in your career when pioneering is practically the only way to draw special attention to your performance. "Getting there fustest with the mostest" is still a success formula for business. Obviously, this kind of operation at your level is possible only when you are surrounded by a staff which also has extremely fast reaction times. If you are to win, the translation of your policy making into workable procedures will have to beat your competition.

You will still be entirely dependent upon your adeptness in the same old functions of management to implement required actions. The trick now will be to adjust your quick perception and understanding to the more complex series of inputs to your personal "computer" and to a faster printout of directions after you have analyzed these data. Both your internal and external communications will be required to act more quickly and more effectively. It will be necessary for you to devise and keep in mind alternative routes at every checkpoint on your personal PERT/time chart. You can be seriously embarrassed only when you come up against a dead end because you have provided no other avenue. The better a student and practitioner you are of the critical path method (the considered managerial judgment of the best of alternative routes through a PERT/time chart), the higher your marks will be as an executive. This is *not* antithetical to your having, and adhering to, a clearly defined personal business philosophy. What it does mean is that there must be a network of roads, all of which lead to Rome.

Building these new procedures into your organizational life will occupy a major part of the training activity you will expend on your subordinates. There is no way for them to know of this new requirement unless you communicate it clearly and with enough reinforcement to insure that all those who work for you get the message, and pronto!

All this can easily result in increased stress and tension for you, unless you actively and continually guard against it. The water skier soon learns that the secret of mastering his sport is to relax, to become nearly as fluid as the medium he is traversing. Many people say that along with superior performance always goes high production of adrenaline by your body and that every winner is under extreme tension. Let us make a careful distinction here. The champion is relaxed; the occasional winner emerges under body- and soul-racking pressure. You are now ready to enter an arena of champions as a peer, and your sojourn there will be painfully short and unrewarding unless you are prepared to compete with them on equal terms. The rapid reaction time we have been urging you to cultivate can never be the continuing product of a body and mind under unendurable pressure. It must in every sense be reflexive, rather than the calculated result of extra effort by your whole system.

Remember that from this point forward, you will be guided by personal motivation almost exclusively in the category of what Abraham Maslow calls self-actualization. Your personal growth must be continual if you are to be effective. The things that worked for you a year or two ago will no longer do so, except for the most fundamental and unalterable principles by which you live. It is the techniques that will be altered to fit a changing environment. One of the quandaries of a technological civilization is the possibility of losing sight of this eternal verity: Human behavior may fluctuate wildly; human nature is as enduring as the hills. Anchor your thinking to this rock as you prepare to make the transition into the atmosphere of the mountain peak; breathing will at times be difficult enough, without complicating it by unnecessary and strength-sapping gymnastics. Save your energy for the ongoing and inescapable drains of daily living, and refuse to be trapped into a useless expenditure of effort.

How Well Do You Read Others' Motives?

It is continually amazing that we know so little about the motivation of those with whom we come in contact. We accept what they do in their relationships with us with few questions about what lies behind their actions or what their goals are. At the same time, we are continually aware of what we want from our peers, and we spend most of our waking moments conniving to get our way from others. Nor does it often occur to us that they may be wondering what makes us tick and planning their strategy to counteract what we are striving for.

The importance of being able to read the motivations of others would be hard to overemphasize. If we know what their goals are, we can make much more intelligent decisions about our own actions. The basic decision to make is whether we give them a hand toward their objectives or strive to prevent their arrival at safe harbor. We will of necessity be either with them or against them individually.

You will naturally have great difficulty in understanding the motivation of others until you have a well-developed concept of the theory of personal motivation. Once you understand what makes people in general behave as they do, you have a reasonable chance of reading the objectives of those with whom you come in contact. It is strongly recommended that you refer to the writings of Douglas McGregor, Abraham Maslow, Frederick Herzberg, Chris Argyris, and Victor Vroom. A synthesis of their ideas can give you helpful guidance. Your basic objective will be to find a way to gain insight into the thoughts and goals of others. Your welfare is inextricably intermeshed with the actions of your associates; only when you know what they want will you be able to make viable decisions about your own actions.

If the general tenor of this chapter seems negative, so be it. We are looking at the situation wherein you are the target for today, and this will put you into a defensive posture. Football championships have been won on the premise that the best offense is an impenetrable defense. If your opponents can't score, the worst that can happen to you is a scoreless tie, and at least you'll never lose.

Remember that your strategy here, for the most part, is to ignore what your opponents say and to concentrate on their nonverbal cues and on what they do. These are the things that count. Your announced enemies pose little problem; it is the ambushers who can give you trouble. They have the dual advantage of anonymity and concealment. You can suffer grievous wounds before you root them from their hiding places, and there is always the possibility that they will run away before you ever identify them.

You have to your advantage the fact that the brush shooter is in general motivated by only a few drives. The first and deepest is jealousy of your position on the heights. He would shoot at anyone occupying the driver's seat, whatever his personality. This trait has a compensatory weakness: Its symptoms always surface eventually, with the result that you can identify your foe. The chances are better than even that he is not in the running as a competitor.

He is probably totally unqualified to occupy your executive seat; his position in the faceless ranks protects him only until he tips his hand. He has another bad habit: He is likely to be undiscriminating about the charges he levels against you, and many of them will be defensible from the start.

The second drive of the ambusher is revenge. Although technically qualified to handle the job to which you have been elevated, he has for one or more reasons been unable to attract the right kind of backing. His political organization may have been ineffective or improperly organized, or he may have had personality conflicts with his superior or others in the executive echelon. Whatever the reasons, he has not been tabbed, and it appears to him that the only way open to him is to attack wildly all those around him, hoping that their destruction will gain him the throne by default.

We should never totally discount the possibility that you have some enemies in the executive ranks. Perhaps your elevation was the result of a split decision, and those who voted "nay" are determined that their vote will eventually be vindicated. By the same token, a disgruntled subordinate may be the guilty party. Rightly or wrongly, he may suspect you of personal wrongdoing; his understandable defense would be to mount an attack upon you.

In the long run, it is immaterial who was involved in the attack against you. The important thing is to organize your defenses at the earliest possible moment and to neutralize the charges by proving their inherent falsity. Keeping your guard up is the most basic tenet in the lexicon of self-defense. From this point forward, you can never afford to remain unguarded for a single instant.

Your job at this juncture is to be alert to every signal being sent. You will have to analyze, sift, reject, and assign priorities to all the data at your command. Speed is of the essence. You will then swing into action with every weapon at your command, but you must be on target. You would never be forgiven for injuring an innocent bystander in this situation.

Basic to this entire thesis is the assumption that you are innocent of all the charges leveled against you. If there is the slightest hint of truth to any of them, your only defense is immediate capitulation and full confession.

How Much Do You Personalize Attacks?

Your chances of emerging unscathed from an attack will be much higher if you can remain completely impersonal about the whole thing. Try to remember that those who are after you probably do not bear you any ill will. You are a symbol, an object, in the way of their achievement of a particular goal, because you are where you are. Every time you allow yourself to feel personal enmity toward an opponent you will be diminishing your effectiveness dangerously. Your thinking and judgment will be impaired. Personal bias will make it impossible for you to see things as they really are, and you are likely to make a poor decision. Your analytical powers will deteriorate, since you will see your enemy as you think he is, rather than as he actually is. If selective perception takes over, you will be in danger of losing out in the encounter.

Naturally, it takes a high degree of self-control to maintain this much objectivity. Self-control has always been a factor of no mean importance in your supervisory and managerial life; as an executive, you can never allow yourself the luxury of letting go—at least in public. In this regard the Japanese have a great idea; they keep crockery rooms for the express purpose of allowing employees to go in and break as much cheap chinaware as it takes to relieve their tensions and hostility. But it is done in private, and there are no witnesses to personal excesses of emotionalism. You are a normal human being, with a full complement of human emotions. But your situation and the scrutiny to which you will be subjected unendingly when you are an executive make certain little personal luxuries no longer possible. Perhaps your subordinates and your peers would be delighted to see you lose control, because it would be evidence of how human you really are, but such a display would lessen their respect for you. That respect is one of your principal assets, and it must not be brushed aside lightly.

If you find yourself in danger of mentally attaching horns to your image of an adversary, the only safe procedure is to take no action until you are certain you have yourself under control. Anything done impulsively now would most surely come out wrong. When you were a first-line supervisor, you learned that you could not afford to hear a grievance or administer discipline without taking advantage of a cooling-off period of a day or two. The same general principle applies when you are under attack now. You can afford to act only when you are certain of your coolness and objectivity. More than likely, your enemy's tactics have in part been predicated upon his ability to make you angry enough to lose control. When that happens, he has you on the run and he knows it.

Another danger in personalizing an attack is that you may credit the instigator with more ability or strength than he has, and thereby possibly develop a defeatist attitude. No one likes to be hated or attacked. Since the average man thinks of himself secretly as a pretty good guy, it is disturbing to his self-image to learn that someone is after him.

One factor of the situation itself makes it all but impossible to exclude personalities entirely. You are being shot at either for weaknesses your detractors see in you or for the abuse of strength. To keep your perspective here, push the reasoning process one step back. Really, you are the target because of what you are doing, not because of what you are. If you can defend to yourself the decisions you are making and the procedures you are using, the personal aspects of the conflict will sink back to a normal configuration, rather than be blown up out of proportion.

There could be value here in pursuing a little more deeply the possibility of some personality changes being forced upon you when you become an executive. You cannot allow yourself to *seem* to be as warm and outgoing as you might like to be. You are the administrator of some impressive sums of money, both for your employees and for your stockholders. The general public has deep distrust for an executive who appears to act impulsively in any area, since they reason that this behavior might be extended into fiscal matters. You will have to make yourself unavailable to many people, including some old friends and co-workers, no matter how foreign this is to your nature. You will be forced to speak in platitudes and clichés in many situations where you wish you could be much more explicit. You must maintain an outward appearance of being extremely hard to sell, even in some areas where you have deep personal convictions already.

In an opposite vein, when you are an executive it will be mandatory at times to maintain all outward appearances of affability and friendliness toward some people with whom you would never have associated before. Unfortunately, most of the time you will have no opposite number with whom to share these unpleasant aspects of your job.

The engineering work—or plastic surgery—necessary to produce this new personality in you has been called the executive mask. Any negative changes your responsibility may force you to display in public do not have to become a part of you. You are still your own man so far as your personal character and feelings are concerned, and you always will be. Not everyone can live this kind of personal dichotomy successfully, and that is why executives are chosen with such painstaking care by those in charge. It is expensive, distasteful, and embarrassing to make a mistake in the choice of an executive, and the top team members live in dread of being thought of as amateurs by their subordinates. One more time, then: Do you really want this kind of job to finish out your working career? There is no room for uncertainty in this personal decision.

How Do You Respond to Hostility?

There are several ways in which a normal adult may respond to aggression or hostility from others. The manner he chooses will be typical of the dominant elements of his personality, and the response to hostility tends to become habitual as he matures. Most frequently, we respond to hostility with hostility. This is the most dysfunctional reaction for the prospective executive, because it gives the advantage of action to the initiator of the aggression and places the man at the receiving end in the position of second-guessing his actions and trying to counter his gambits. You have little chance to exhibit any initiative or originality in this situation.

The second most common response is to try to avoid any contact with the aggressor and thereby escape unharmed. This reaction consumes a great deal of energy, and most executives hesitate to adopt it even though it might be highly effective. The reluctance to evade the issue arises from a possible misinterpretation of the action by onlookers. Their first thought would be that cowardice was a motivator for the executive. The fact that his decision to avoid the aggressor might have been actuated by his desire to protect his group from an all-out battle would be hard to sell to the troops.

A third possible reaction to hostility or aggression is to freeze within a protective shell and refuse to show any response at all. As an executive, you will have a well-organized system of defenses against encroachments. There is, first, the prestige and status of your position; the fact that you are where you are is in itself one of your better defenses. Second, most organizations have at the executive level two or more rings of subordinates who make access to you all but impossible if you so order it. Third, you could pretend complete ignorance of attack from any quarter. This response is one of the most frustrating to your enemy. No one likes to be ignored, and when a man is intent on a vendetta, he can hardly stand to be made to look like Don Quixote tilting at windmills. The effectiveness of this consider-the-source attitude on the part of the executive is usually dependent upon the position of the attacker. If your foe is a level or two below you in the hierarchy, or is an outsider, you have a better than even chance of success if you behave as if nothing out of the ordinary was occurring. If your enemy is at your own level or higher, either in or out of your organization, you might want to consider the matter carefully before trying to ignore it.

The fourth and perhaps generally most effective method of responding to hostility is a combination of the first three. For example, you might elect to maintain a public posture of ignoring what is going on, while mounting a counteraggression behind the scenes. In this way, those close to you who know what is really happening will be satisfied that you are doing something about it, and at the same time they will admire you for maintaining your composure in public. Concurrently, your enemy would be aware that you are a worthy foe, since he would be feeling the results of your own aggressive tactics. The scars of the executive who uses this approach are smaller and disappear more quickly.

It would be unfortunate if this chapter were to elicit a response at either extreme of the spectrum we have described. The life of the executive is not totally caught up in conflict, nor is it ever completely peaceful. You will always have degrees of involvement in altercations with others, ranging from minor irritants to all-out war that will of course absorb your total attention and energy.

As an executive, you will have much more autonomy

in choosing your course of action than you have ever enjoyed before. When you become skipper of your craft, you also assume control over the navigator's function. Moreover, you will have sources of information at your hand which will give greater breadth and depth to your understanding of the entire scene, thus enabling you to render better judgments than you could when you were lower down on the ladder. Essentially, your future is now much more firmly in your hands, and whether you succeed or fail will ultimately depend on actions of your choice.

To keep things in perspective, we should remark one fact: Few men or women are attracted to an executive position unless they are highly competitive. Such people enjoy a real thrill in the contest for its own sake, and they quite easily become totally involved in a test of strength. For their self-actualization, they must prove repeatedly that they are at least competitive with the champion and that they have a right to be in the arena with him. This is one of the higher nonfinancial rewards of the executive's job and has been the continuing motivator for many leaders in business and industry. By nature, the executive has a greater capacity for producing and tolerating adrenaline in the bloodstream than does the typical follower.

Every time you become the object of another's hostility will be unique and will require your full powers of analysis before you choose your response to it. You will have to make the final decision as to how you will respond when you become the target. No one else can know both the situation and you as well as you do. Again, this is part of the essential and continuing loneliness of the executive.

What Is Your Level of Self-confidence?

If you accept the thesis that the executive is a lonely man, you must also conclude that he is going to have to depend upon his own resources almost entirely in his business dealings. He may, and does, have many others to turn to for advice, but the final decisions will be his, and he must take full responsibility and accountability for them. This fact presupposes that the successful top manager has a full measure of self-confidence; if he did not, he would undergo too much anxiety to continue to function in his position.

As a leader now, and as an executive candidate, you must be inner-directed. Your natural tendency is to rely upon yourself, rather than to take orders from anyone else if you can avoid it. Only a fairly small percentage of us feel comfortable in this situation. Most of us are more at ease when others are responsible for directing our efforts; we are not inner-directed, and happy that way, because of the lighter load of responsibility we carry. If our enterprise fails, we can rationalize that the failure is not ours, but that of our leadership. You, as an executive candidate, must think differently. You must have an ongoing deep conviction that you can make the right decisions, that you can pick the right people for the various positions, and that you can then lead and direct them successfully.

A high level of self-confidence grows from an accumulation of successful actions during your business career. Every time you make a correct decision, you add another brick to the wall of your belief in your ability as a businessman. This is good. We harp so much on the necessity of learning from our mistakes that we sometimes neglect the fact that we also learn much from our successes—or should. We assume that each decision has been arrived at through a logical process; when that logic is shown to be correct, we should be ready to use it again in similar situations in the future.

Self-confidence is not a monolithic structure; it is composed of several discrete parts. You must believe in your process of reasoning. You must feel that your decisions about money and finance will stand the test of time and events. Also, you must have confidence when you pick your people, and you must be able to work with them smoothly on a continuing basis. You must have unshakable confidence in your own integrity and ability to survive attacks upon it, both the spurious external attacks designed to overthrow you, and the more insidious temptations which will be put in your way repeatedly by those who wish to use you.

Most important of all, your self-confidence should be strong enough not to be shaken when you do make errors. Remember, you will be lucky or superhuman if you bat higher than 58 to 60 percent in the decisions you make as an executive. Since those decisions will have so much more impact than your former ones did, you can expect severe personal upset when one goes sour. If you allow this reaction seriously to undermine your self-confidence, you will be on the way out. There will always be people to remind you of your mistakes; most of your successes will be taken for granted and go unremarked by those same people. Your self-confidence must, then, be intrinsically reinforcing. Self-confidence and self-control are Siamese twins; they can only exist together, and they aid and abet each other's growth and strength.

One professional bowler who was successful for a number of years claimed publicly that he practiced self-hypnosis as one of his tools for consistently high performance. It might be interesting to try this technique as a method of reinforcing your self-confidence. Any clinical psychologist could teach you this procedure. The objective is not to fool yourself—it is simply to increase your concentration on sustaining a high level of belief in your abilities, both innate and developed. You will need every bit of bolstering you can get from all sources to give you the strength to carry through your duties as an executive.

*   *   *

This chapter has been devoted to an analysis of your reaction to, and possible protection from, attack by your enemies when you become an executive. You will not at first be accustomed to the frequency or strength of these attacks. You must refuse to panic; it is better to take no action at all, at first, than to become panicky.

But you can't remain a standing target for long without being hurt. By carefully selected training, you can improve your reaction time significantly. But a quick response is useless unless you also exercise good judgment and make valid decisions to buttress your proposed actions. Your actions must have purpose if they are to be viable.

You will do far better if you refuse to personalize attacks upon you; otherwise, too much emotionalism and rancor will cloud your ability to make a proper choice of counteraction. By the same token, you must closely control your response to hostility. You cannot afford to return hostility with hostility in every situation. Too much is at stake to fall into that trap.

It is important to your survival that you be able to read the motives of those around you quickly and well. If you know what their objectives are, you have a much better chance of anticipating their future actions as they concern you.

Finally, you must have rich resources of self-confidence to give you strength when you are under attack. If you don't believe in yourself, you can't expect others to follow your leadership. Your position is a desirable one, but you must assiduously cultivate methods of defending yourself from attack if you want to hold your gains.

6

How Good
Is Your Crystal Ball?

MORE than a touch of mysticism still plays a role in management. Almost every day the average manager is required to make one or more educated guesses rather than a decision he can defend logically. This situation arises partly from the fact that he cannot always get immediate data and partly from our inability to quantify human behavior. When he is working in the human side of management, there will be many occasions when he must make and support intuitive judgments. However, in the part of his job that employs less-than-scientific methods, the executive must have better-than-average talent to discover trends early, significantly ahead of the general public.

Can You Spot Trends Before They Are Obvious?

The fact that this is largely a matter of personal sensitivity does not mean that you are prohibited from using your best powers of analysis in forecasting developing currents. In fact, the marketing manager spends much of his time in exactly this procedure. He will stand or fall on his continuing ability to predict where the sales will be, in what volume, and for what products. Similarly, the executive in general management must recognize a latent problem, plan for coping with it, and implement a course of action to go along with trends when they are still not generally recognized.

This intuitive process is not as esoteric as it might sound at first. To be productive, intuition must be the result of deep and extensive knowledge of a specialized area; it will mature only after years of carefully observed experience of the right sort. If you are by nature a methodical person, you might profit from keeping charts showing the periodicity of the rise and fall of a given characteristic of a particular business. However, these charts are generally of little value unless you make a serious effort to account for variations in all the identifiable independent variables that have an effect on the trait in which you are interested. You will actually be studying and following the changes in the factor whose trends have an interest for you. You are, in other words, attempting to become an authority in a given aspect of your business.

The person who stands to gain most spectacularly from real expertise in this process is the entrepreneur. Many of the world's great fortunes have been founded on what many people attribute to lucky guesses. To say the least, this is a debatable premise. It is more likely that the entrepreneur saw quite clearly the developments from which he could profit if he prepared himself.

This does not mean that an executive in a public corporation will find the same characteristic any less valuable. He can make himself a real champion even by spotting only a few emerging trends over the years. It is true that with increasingly swift obsolescence becoming the order of the day, he will be called upon to make more frequent trend analyses than he was in the past. The order used to be: Take good care of your bread-and-butter items, and have a pot simmering on the back burner. This has now been changed: Turn the bread-and-butter item over to the most junior executive, concentrate your efforts on the products you intend to release tomorrow, and make research and development accountable for the bright gewgaws due out in a year or two. As a practicing executive, you will probably delegate a part of this trend-seeking activity to one or more of your better staff members, but you dare not ever let yourself become too remote from the center of the action. It is too important to your overall responsibility as a manager of change for your enterprise. You will become preeminent in your field in direct ratio to your continuing ability to originate much of that change.

As you begin to fit yourself into the executive's job, you will discover the excitement of smelling out new trends. This is a contest which pits you against the world. It goes without saying that there are many other contestants in the arena with you—your competitors. In the business world there are countless examples of rival companies that hit the market with nearly identical products within weeks or even days of each other. To the trained observer, the significant indicators are there to be seen and followed. A few years ago in the pharmaceutical industry, the notebooks of researchers in all major companies had to be notarized at the end of each working day. Basic patents can be granted or denied on the judgment of a few hours' difference in timing.

It will be your responsibility to gain the personal experience and expertise which will form the basis for this very special ability to spot trends. No one else can do this for you. Actually, you have been doing this all your years in management. Now is the time for you to reap some of the benefits of that preparation. You will find many of the higher rewards of your job in your ability to make accurate and profitable forecasts of developing trends. To obtain the best results for the entire group, you should disclose your reasoning to a select number of your closer associates well in advance of implementation of your plan. The fact that you are pioneering does not mean you can do without independent judgments as to the validity of your conclusions. You will need the help of your subordinates downstream, and it will help them a great deal if you allowed them a gestation period for conceptualizing the general idea. Remember, you are now most certainly a leader, but you are the leader of a team. Your followers will have to be prepared for the comfortable introduction to a new aspect of your enterprise.

Can You Read Your Competition?

One of the more important areas in which you must be sensitive is that of guessing what your competition is up to. We hear much these days of industrial espionage and all the proprietary secrets that are sold for hard cash by venal employees. Unquestionably, some of this goes on, but the advantages gained in this way are a long way from equaling those that are the product of close observation, good reasoning, accumulated knowledge of the business in general, and—once in a while—a dash of extra good luck. Seemingly miraculous things can happen when you play the game, What would I do if I were president of Brand X?, where Brand X is, of course, your closest competitor. This exercise should be a daily activity. You know exactly what you are going to do, so what would your strategy be if you were your rival and had a pretty good idea of your plans? It is similar to playing chess alone, especially if you put some thought and extra effort into the moves of your opponent.

Since you are not a mind reader, you will immediately discover that your opposite number at Brand X has several alternatives at each stage of activity. Your strategy can then be planned around the countermoves you would take to the alternatives he might select. It is not unusual for a large company to have a good-size long-range planning group that lays out procedures for every conceivable modus operandi that can be dreamed up for the competition wherever it may be or whatever its size and strength. Even nowadays, when industries spring out of nowhere as if by magic, it is not impossible for one good product, or a new twist on a service, to nurture an industrial or business giant. Competitors can emerge and pass you overnight unless you are alert.

Your role as an executive in this situation is that of idea man, stimulator, or catalyst. You should not be trapped by the fascination of this game into spending too much time second-guessing what Brand X will or will not do. Too many other problems demand your attention. A fairly steady stream of short memos to the subordinates to whom you have delegated this function should be your input. Let them do the worrying and the legwork about the details. Their feedback can keep you adequately up to date.

Clearly, one key to your success here is a broad and documented general knowledge of the top personnel among your important business rivals. This is one reason for the noticeable fraternization among executives of all the companies in a given industry. All of them are recording in their memory banks various bits of data for use now or in the future. This is a perfectly legitimate pastime; each one knows what the others are doing, and no one has any guilt about it.

We have already noted the similarity of this activity to chess. Perhaps we could change the analogy now and bring in poker. There are two strategies you should always be on the alert for among the players: bluffing and the false signal. Since they are executives, like you, they will be employing the same techniques in thinking of you. Some of the many moves your rivals make will be deliberately contrived to misinform you and lead you down the garden path. You will have to be particularly hardnosed in your analysis of anything you learn about their activities, especially those planned for the future. Is there logic in what you have heard they are planning? Do they have the capital to finance the necessary facilities for a major move? What about their managerial depth? Is there someone already in the organization capable of being project chief for an entirely new product? What is the reputation of their research and development department, and have new people been added to that staff lately?

If the answers to these questions do not add up to a significant number of pluses, chances are that you have been lured on with an attractive red herring. Many times it takes more nerve *not* to react than it does to plunge into all-out action. You, as the involved executive, will have to make this decision.

We have used the word "intuition" several times. As the businessman uses the term in both his thinking and his actions, there is a little mysticism involved, but a lot more shortcut logic. During his years in the field, he has built a pyramid of data. When a given situation closely resembles another he recalls from his past, he remembers his decisions and his actions then, as well as the results. If, in his judgment, the two situations are quite similar, he is likely, in the interests of saving time, to omit one or more steps in the decision-making process and to announce a couple of usable alternatives as if he had really pulled them out of thin air. The higher you progress in the hierarchy, the more valuable time becomes; any of it you can save for both yourself and your company will be reflected in the profit and loss statement. There will always be an element of risk in making decisions in this manner; it is your job as an executive to minimize this risk by backing up your projected actions with the best possible use of your experience.

So, when asked whether you can read your competition, you must consider all these factors before giving your answer. It is of prime importance to your success to be able to do so. Few of the elements that go into such a reading will be learned after you become an executive; you have spent a business lifetime gathering them and making them your own. It is how you use them now that will count. The communications aspect of this process will be considered separately later, since it looms large in this picture.

In your new job you will be required to be highly sensitive in dealing both with people and with things. These two components of the business scene are not separable; they will continue to share equal billing in your work for the rest of your career.

How Good Are You at Choosing People?

If there is any one area in your job situation where your crystal ball will be needed, it is in the matter of selecting personnel. Anyone of potential executive caliber knows well that his decisions about people are much more difficult to make, and much less predictable in outcome, than are his decisions about things. In fact, if only the latter were involved, there would be no more need for supervision. Modern technology is so advanced that a computer and a trained technician could make all the necessary decisions about things.

Most executives find it highly frustrating to realize that they have made relatively little progress in selecting good people since their earliest days in supervision. In the first place, there are so many independent variables at work in a human personality that no formula can be developed for evaluating personality and intrinsic human potential. Until we come to know a man or woman personally over an extended period of time, no instrument can even come close to quantifying or evaluating qualities such as honesty and integrity. Every businessman is inevitably led to the conclusion that he will have to be guided more by his intuition than by any other single factor in choosing his personnel.

The second reason for the executive's feeling of frustration is that he is interacting with some of the more intelligent, motivated, ambitious, and smoothly operating people on the business scene. If the applicant is reasonably smart, he will know the "best" answers to the questions so artlessly being fired at him.

Nevertheless, some areas in evaluating personnel do approach a level of objectivity. The candidate's record can be studied to measure the results he has achieved, and you can take soundings from trusted associates as to their impressions of the person in question. You might also find it desirable to undertake carefully a small amount of peer evaluation to balance and round out your data. Despite all this, however, your ultimate judgment about a prospective subordinate will be in every respect a value estimate of your own.

Your past record probably demonstrates your better-than-average ability to put the right person into the right spot. If not, you would not have been outstanding enough to become a candidate for the executive echelon. However, you may not be able to verbalize the method you used to accomplish this feat because, as indicated, it is basically a product of your intuition.

We cannot avoid an examination of one of the less pleasant aspects of the executive job. Fairly frequently, you will find it necessary to devise and administer to your associates what cannot honestly be called anything but tests. There is something innately degrading in treating a person as if he were a sample of raw chemicals. Nevertheless, there is no other valid method by which you, the executive, can make anything like a reasonable discrimination between two candidates of similar strengths. You are trying to determine the winner between two close contestants. The competitors usually recognize what you are doing, and, if you can demonstrate a lack of bias in your judgment of results, the loser will not bear you any ill will. He knows the paramount importance to the enterprise of having the best possible man in each slot. He also knows that if you make a wrong choice, failure is the likely result for the man picked, and that would be highly undesirable.

Another complication in this matter of selecting working associates is the fact that your future as well as theirs is in the balance. Nowhere is there more truth than in the statement that a manager rises or falls on the caliber of his people. The manner in which they carry out your directives, and the results they achieve, will determine your results and your reputation in their entirety. Herewith, another warning to you when you become an executive: Do not let this knowledge throw you into a mental tailspin to the point where you become defensive and then postpone indefinitely necessary personnel decisions. Do your homework; take a reasonable time for reflection; then make your decision and relax. You will be either right or wrong. This is one area in which little gray beclouds the issue. The final judgment will be rendered in black or white.

Obviously, this matter of selecting personnel is one of the more severe pressure spots in the life of an executive. This fact should trigger what is by now nearly a conditioned response: your own most viable way of reducing that pressure to manageable proportions. After you have wrestled with and, we hope, won a decision, remove yourself from the business scene for a few days to ponder. You are now more important to the enterprise than you have ever been before and are no longer living only for yourself and your family. A host of other people now depend upon your expertise in many areas for their general well-being. You owe it to them—and to yourself—to be at the peak of your performance in all situations and to realize your personal potential to the full. This is one aspect of that increased responsibility you indicated your willingness to undertake when you announced your candidacy for an executive's job. You have few superiors any more to pass judgment on your performance; rather, it is now the entire enterprise, and this is an awesome responsibility.

Can You Forecast the Situation?

Many of your most important decisions as an executive will require you to understand the complicated relationships among products, people, and environment both inside and outside the company. Seldom, in fact, will you be able to simplify a problem enough to consider only one of its components. Each component of every situation in modern society is becoming more complex every day, and the total mix is infinitely more so. Actually, you have become significantly more astute in your perceptions, in your ability to analyze them, and in the practice of proposing appropriate action in the years since you entered supervision. If this were not true, you would not have survived to become a manager and a prospective executive.

Now we are asking you to develop the ability to forecast how the situation in your enterprise may be expected to change, and in what direction, over the coming months and years. This will be much more than a crystal-ball exercise. You will need access to and interpretation of every kind of indicator and barometer that modern management has to offer, many and varied as they are. Learn to throw into the pot for analysis a yeasty and fluid new kind of workforce, the requirements of a much more sophisticated product market, and an economy which now transcends national boundaries and will continue to do so.

Because it is clear that forecasting will always be empirical, your first and continuing need will be for a body of historical data to serve as a bench mark against which to measure the new facts as they are printed out for you. By all means give this activity the highest short-term priority while you wait for your promotion. Ask yourself what the climate will be 90 days from now for sales, production, quality, or labor relations. Feed in all pertinent data you can scrape up, and crank out your prediction. Then try to keep from gnawing your fingernails until the red-marked day on the calendar rolls around.

Did your prediction miss the mark? If you were significantly off target, analyze intensively the entire process you used to make your forecast and pinpoint the soft spots. Do you need to add some new indicators, or were you working from insufficient data on those already in service? Of major importance for your personal information is this question: Were you overly optimistic or pessimistic in your predictions? You must know this in order to make an adjustment in sighting your target the next time around. When you have two or three resounding successes in short-term forecasting, stretch out the time increment. Double it, say, to six months, then to a year.

This will be the most complicated business game you have undertaken to play so far, and by all odds the most challenging. Assuredly, this will not be a one-man activity. You will find it necessary to get the cooperation not only of every member of your staff, but also of those in many other disciplines. Level with your colleagues. If you tell them what you are doing, you will probably arouse their interest and elicit their wholehearted commitment.

You should also recheck closely the state of readiness of your proposed replacement. Do you feel really confident about his ability to take over your reins? This question is of much more than academic interest, since you are not about to go anywhere until you have a demonstrably ready successor. New blood can always be brought into the company as the result of an executive search, but holes in the thinning and stretched ranks of middle management are desperately hard to plug satisfactorily. To do so is your responsibility.

It would be enlightening here to stop and count the people whom you have involved, accidentally or by design, in your own development leading toward your next promotion. The total will be impressive. Because of the esoteric nature of some of the disciplines you are now becoming familiar with, there are a lot of strangers in the crew. That is, they were strangers until a few months ago. By involving them in your personal growth process, you have markedly widened your associations both inside and out-

side your company. This can only be good. The more people you know in a working relationship before you become
an executive, the more allies you will have when their
goodwill becomes so terribly important to you. Never
underestimate the value of a gang behind you, if for nothing more than the psychological lift it gives you when the
going gets a little tough.

Notice also how much less ritualized and specific your
development program has become in this last phase. More
than ever, it is intimately associated with aspects of your
present job and is more job-oriented. You may not have
thought about attending an outside seminar for many
months, since there have been so many fascinating projects
tangential to your regular job which need your attention.
What you are undergoing is true manager development.

How Good Is Your Conceptual Skill?

The elements which make up conceptual skill are sensitivity, precise observation, and the ability to see associations between things which are not obviously related. As
an executive, you are going to need every shred of this skill
that you can command, since your job will be to conceptualize the actions and progress of your enterprise. Many
people develop a mental block against conceptualization,
because they think of it as a personality factor which is
innate and not trainable. Nothing could be further from
the truth. You can train yourself in conceptualization; in
fact, you have been doing so for several months or years
while mastering your middle management job and starting
to look toward another promotion.

127

We have already outlined one excellent training device for developing conceptual skill: your exercise in forecasting the situation in your area for the near future. That process represents a master drawing for any type of conceptualizing activity you will ever undertake. You can readily transfer the techniques to other areas of your job and repeat the process, to help you generalize in this skill. The important thing is that you cause it to happen, rather than wait for it to happen.

Gaining expertness in conceptualizing will give you some of the greatest self-satisfaction you will ever achieve in your job. As we have said, the activity must be planned and guided, and you will spend much time and effort in gathering pertinent data. But somewhere along the line will come an extremely pleasurable flash of insight. A large part of this satisfaction lies in the realization that you are making a definitive and significant contribution to the success of your venture. Here is something unique, which no one has ever done before in your organization.

No true skill in conceptualizing can ever be achieved by limiting your work to internal considerations. To see the entire picture, you will need to acquire knowledge of all the independent variables which deeply affect your company from the outside. That is why the modern executive must be an expert about his entire industry and must know how that industry fits into the general economy, on both a national and an international basis. You are now a citizen of the world, since more and more major industries are transcending national boundaries in scope and interactions.

At this point, it is imperative that you make some sort of measurement of the present state of your expertness in this category. Granted, it is only recently that your job has required anything at all in this field, and your body of personal historical data is sparse; nevertheless, you have to draw up a balance sheet to get a rough idea of your totem-pole position in this skill. Your rivals for promotion have had the same constraints and limitations on their performance, so you are starting equal in every respect. The only possible advantage any of them can have over you is their earlier awareness of the necessity, which means that they may have gotten an earlier start in developing conceptualization skills. To allow this to happen is to handicap yourself severely in the race for the laurel.

The measurement mentioned is not difficult. Evidences of skill are immediately apparent to the interested observer. Behind every major success in a project undertaken at the upper-middle management or executive level, there will be better-than-average conceptualization of the problem and the real objectives for the group. This is a *sine qua non*. You can no longer gallop off in all directions in a fury of activity the moment you receive a cue that action is required. Action must be considered, as it must be in a specific direction. It is much better to allow a period of time for reasoning out your attack before starting the action. The results will be better if you do.

The fact that you are responsible for being aware of all the implications of what is going on certainly does not imply that this is a one-man show. If ever you needed the help of all your team members, it is now.

This mental set will bring you many personal benefits. When you begin to look at your job from the broader viewpoint, you will inevitably do the same thing in other aspects of your life, which will be enriched in direct proportion to how far you push this outlook. Anyone who is sincere and conscientious in his work is in great danger of developing tunnel vision. He concentrates so much on the here and now that he has no time or thought for what is going on around him or for the many and complex factors which complicate and enrich the entire scene. You have been operating more and more as a generalist as you progressed up the hierarchy. Instead of treating this as an unwelcome necessity, you should adopt it eagerly as a way of life and exploit it to the full. The end result of doing a superior job for your employer should be a richer, fuller, and more complete personal life for you, with refinements and enjoyments you never dreamed of a few years ago.

A great executive must also be a person of great spirit. Now, with your wider and deeper responsibilities, and your influence on so many more people, you truly have an unparalleled opportunity to make a real contribution to a significant segment of society. To be successful, your business must satisfy needs through either a product or a service. Naturally, there should be a profit in it for you, but the profit will be measured in many ways other than the purely financial. Right now, if you concentrate on developing your ability to conceptualize, you will be opening the door to a future new in many of its best aspects.

How Do You Communicate Your Reading?

No amount of sensitivity, no amount of meticulous observation, no unique perception, and no number of logical syntheses on your part can be functional in your organization unless you communicate effectively with those around you. There is a commonly held fallacy that as a person climbs in the hierarchy he becomes more independent of those around him. Actually, the exact opposite is true. The middle manager has less real latitude of action than does the first-line foreman, and the executive finds himself relying more on the goodwill and cooperation of his subordinates than does any other manager. He gets his work done through other people. How are they going to know what you want them to do unless you tell them?

The objective of this communicative process is to help your subordinates develop their conceptual powers, as well as to simply get the work of the moment accomplished. Your goal is to weld an effective team which will attain your objectives ahead of your peers and your rivals for promotion. The building of your team will require two kinds of communicative effort on your part: the regular, routine, stand-up report meetings you hold with your staff and any special efforts a given project may require. It would be difficult to prove that either activity is more important than the other. To get the job done, you are going to have to do both exceptionally well.

The surest signal of an ineffective group is frequent complaints of your staff members that they are not getting the word. It is also a sign of a breakdown in morale. If for any reason you decide to withhold a bit of information they would like to have, it is your clear duty to tell them so and, if possible, to tell them the reason why you are not communicating that item. That probably will not completely satisfy them, but it will at least ease the pain a little.

Nor should you ever forget that true communication is a closed loop. You have to listen to your people as much as they have to hear what you say. Although the executive lives a life of isolation, he can needlessly exaggerate that isolation, and thereby reduce his effectiveness, if he fails to hear the cues sent his way by those working with him. In your business activity, bits of information are usually complementary, and they may be meaningless unless they are read together. Of great importance to the communicative cycle is, of course, the attitudes of both sender and receiver. We already have enough barriers and filters to our messages without complicating the matter by being the slightest bit unreceptive to them. Never be too proud or afraid to admit that you don't understand what someone is telling you.

The greatest aid, or the biggest and most impenetrable barrier, to true communication is the presence or absence of complete trust and confidence among those involved. If you have the slightest reason to feel less than total confidence in one member of your group, he has no business being there, and you are committing a grave error so long as you do not rectify this condition.

It is also possible to harm your group by being over-communicative. Part of mutual trust and confidence is your belief that your people know their job and do it well. They have minds of their own and can determine with a high degree of accuracy the important data for their portion of the action. Don't insult their intelligence and undermine their faith in you by patronizing them with worthless data. If they are lacking in minor bits of the picture, trust them to come to you to be filled in. Once again, we must say that the optimal goal is balance in your communication. Give them what they need, including necessary background, and then leave them alone. Communication will take enough of your time, without your having to go overboard.

*   *   *

These pages have been concerned with a part of your job closely related to extrasensory perception. We have put some rather severe tests in the way of your preparation for becoming an executive. Are you able to spot trends before they are clearly visible to the general public? You will have to see connections between apparently unrelated facts and take action according to your interpretation of these relationships. Closely allied to this is your ability to look on the marketplace through the eyes of your competition. The planning of your strategy will be connected with your reading of what your business rivals will be doing downstream.

Because human beings are so infinitely variable, it will never be possible to put the selection of personnel on a scientific basis. There will always be an element of calculated risk when you choose staff members. This does not mean for a moment that you should ignore the records of the various candidates for the jobs you have open; it means only that those records cannot be a definitive factor in the choices you will make.

Another critical aspect of your general sensitivity is your ability to forecast what the situation will be for your business a few months or years from now. All kinds of indicators will go into your consideration of this, but your final guess will be drawn from these component parts.

Your results will be measured hereafter almost entirely on your ability to conceptualize. The impact of your job now is both internal and external. The welfare of your enterprise depends on how well you can see it in relationship to others and to the economy at large.

Finally, all these activities will be useless unless you do just the right amount and kind of communicating with your people. They have a right to know what is going on so that they can do a good job for you.

7

What Is
Your Anxiety Level Now?

OUR working assumption is that you are a normal human being; therefore, the situation in which you now find yourself cannot fail to produce a high level of tension in you. Moreover, there is every prospect that you will have to live with this tension, and its accompanying high level of anxiety, for an indeterminate period. It may be many months, or even years, before you are actually promoted to an executive position. And when you are, you will experience greater stress in your normal working day than ever before. You need to prepare for this stress and once again affirm your decision to pursue your goal. If you find the prospect of this inner turmoil too distasteful, it is better to find it out now than after you have made the move.

How Well Do You Sleep?

One of the surest signs of tension and anxiety is insomnia. For most people, disturbance of long-established sleeping habits adds to their general upset. However, you should not panic about this problem. Physiological and psychological studies of sleep have proved conclusively that people differ widely in their need for sleep and that any given person may require different amounts of sleep at different times. Thus there is no such thing as normal sleeping habits. The key is to determine how much sleep you need and to try to get it.

If you begin to experience difficulty in falling asleep, and if this is a purely psychosomatic response to the pressures of your job and the outlook for the future, there are some things you can do about it. Light exercise, such as walking, just before you retire may help you to fall asleep. Slight physical fatigue often counteracts the mental activity which has been robbing you of your rest. Also, a glass of warm milk may tend to shift some of the blood from your brain to your stomach and increase the probability of getting to sleep within a reasonable time. A combination of these methods might be helpful.

It is another matter when you awaken in the middle of the night. One of the better ways to handle this problem is to do some reading. The nature of the material is critical Choose either a light and soporific book or something so heavy that you can't understand it. Only in dire circumstances should you open your briefcase and dive back into your regular work. The last thing you need now is more of the stimulus which triggered your sleeplessness. If you, like most managers, have worked assiduously for many years to develop self-control, you can perhaps simply will yourself into a state of mental relaxation. If you are successful at this gambit, you may awaken in the morning in your comfortable big chair.

The overall guiding principle for forestalling difficulty and interruptions in your sleep is to establish the most rigorous habits of regularity in your hours for retiring and arising. You probably determined years ago how many hours of sleep you need. Use every method at your command to let nothing interfere with your pattern.

In this matter you can, and should, expect the full cooperation of your family. If you need more sleep than your wife or your older children, they should respect your needs and organize their activities at home so as not to disturb your sleep. This is certainly not to suggest that you become a robot. Some of our most refreshing experiences stem from a deliberate violation of established routine. These are best when they occur spontaneously and for no good reason except that you have a yen to do something different. It is possible under this kind of stimulus to miss most of a night's sleep without feeling excessive fatigue. Of course, such occasions will be relatively widely spaced. Once again, moderation should be your objective.

It is entirely possible that you may undergo your entire middle management experience and your preparation for advancement into the executive echelon without noticeable upset of your sleeping patterns. If so, you are to be congratulated. However, it is much more likely that somewhere along the line you will experience some change in your sleeping habits. To recapitulate: Do not become upset when sleep eludes you; to do so can only compound the problem. By maintaining a rational attitude and a low-keyed approach, you will have a much better chance of either minimizing the problem or causing it to disappear completely.

There are also people who learn to live with continuing insomnia. Some of the world's more successful people have been light sleepers. If this should be your case, learn to keep calm and get the maximum values from whatever sleep does come your way. Some people sleep faster than others.

What Is Your Irritation Flash Point?

We have become accustomed to two generalizations about human beings. The first is that people vary widely in the point at which they sound off from irritation; the second is that any one person can vary from time to time in the level at which he shows fire. Many things contribute to this second factor: physical health at the moment, the number of pressures at the job or at home, the irritability of associates, the weather, the amount of overall tension.

There are a couple of reasons why this is an important issue to you at all times in your managerial career. The first is, of course, your own well-being. If you allow yourself to flare up over details, you will not only put needless wear and tear on your nervous system, but also lower your efficiency. Second, your irritable behavior will affect your associates, especially those working for you. Through experience with you, they have estimated the point at which you may usually be expected to strike out punitively. If you depart radically from that predicted point, you will confuse them badly and add to their tension and dissatis-faction. This is one of the areas in which they much prefer the boss to be predictable.

It may be feasible for you to keep a simple log of the in-cidents which cause you to lose your temper. Be specific, listing contributing factors, the people involved, and a short but fairly complete narrative of what happened. As you accumulate data about these events over a period of time, you can start to make some good observations about the significance of the triggering event. Are you generally becoming shorter-tempered or more even-tempered? Do you suspect that your subordinates sometimes keep things from you because they fear your reaction to particular bits of news?

If you can detect a definitely shorter fuse to your tem-per than you had a year ago, it is time to take some action. This is one of the more certain signs that your job is begin-ning to get to you, and you need to do some serious stock-taking and personal reorientation. Much more is involved here than the smoothness of your interpersonal relation-ships. The effectiveness of your group is going to suffer drastically if you become mean tempered and irritable. At your level, you work with good men who will not stay long around an unreasonable and crotchety leader.

We should make a fine distinction here. No reasonable manager will expect you to assume the character of a Great Stone Face. As a normal human being, you will be expected to react with anger and its physical manifestations when you are seriously provoked. So we are back once more to that old workhorse, self-control. The greater the power and authority you acquire, the greater is your responsibility to behave like a mature adult. Nothing can ruin your reputation as a manager more quickly than to have word get around that you are beginning to act childishly.

At your position in the hierarchy, you have a fine technique at your command if you will but use it. Since you now have much more control of your time, simply disappear for a half day when you find yourself about to blow your stack. Take a long drive in the country, or go fishing in a secluded spot. Dissipate the extra adrenaline with some sort of physical activity, but be sure not to let it take the form of spinning your wheels or striking out at those near at hand. Getting away from work can have other benefits, too. Many times, in a different atmosphere you can come up with a couple of fine new ideas, or solve an old and nagging problem. On your return, your associates will be delighted to see that your entire outlook has brightened and that you seem refreshed and invigorated.

One of the more important aspects of your personal restraint is the effect it will have on your subordinates. Don't forget how much imitation there is among the members of the organization. All of us, consciously or unconsciously, tend to follow the pattern set by a leader we admire. If he is a lid flipper, we may become one also; if he usually exhibits admirable self-control, we find it easier to maintain moderation in our own actions. It is not necessary to discuss this with your people. They will adjust their behavior automatically.

If you begin to lose control of your temper over trifles, you are running a grave risk of lowering your personal efficiency to the danger point, or even below it. You don't have the time or the energy to waste in venting your spleen over personal irritations. This reiteration of a point made earlier is deliberate because of its importance to you. The moment you lose control of yourself, you become immensely more vulnerable because you have then also lost control of the situation. Your enemies would be delighted to find you in this condition, because you would then be a sitting duck.

The trick is to maintain a positive attitude. You have so much going for you, and so little militating against you, that it is ridiculous to react negatively to the little things that go wrong on any given day. To do so is to magnify their importance out of all proportion; you are about to lose your sense of values. Next to your personal integrity, your set of values is your most priceless business possession. It is the stabilizer for the vessel of your career. Maybe, after your next promotion, you will want to install a punching bag in the bathroom of your executive suite; in the meantime, don't make the fatal error of using your associates in that capacity.

How Much Did You Enjoy Your Last Vacation?

Many a manager exhibits every sign of being afraid to take a vacation. He offers weird and wonderful rationalizations by the dozen to explain why he cannot go away for two weeks. He claims that he has too heavy a work load, when everyone in the organization knows he has exercised superb delegation to a smoothly functioning team. Or he says that he must plan for the coming semiannual segment of the budget, or he must be available for a series of coordinating conferences between production and sales, when actually he can contribute little to these meetings but his presence. When pressured from above, or at home, he will grudgingly use his accrued vacation time over a series of long weekends.

At best, there cannot be more than two ultimate reasons for this behavior: Either the manager is so totally committed to his job that he gets no enjoyment from any other activity, or he is afraid to leave for fear that his superiors will draw the wrong conclusion when they see his group functioning well without him.

If either of these reasons is keeping a manager from taking a vacation and enjoying it to the full, he is in bad shape on the job. The truly functional executive is the one who is able to enjoy all the normal activities of life. Of course he is thoroughly involved in his work, and gets huge satisfaction from his accomplishments. But he is also a family man, and the demands of his job put constraints upon his available time for his family. For him, the vacation should be a time for renewing and enriching family ties. Even if his children are grown and gone, as is often the case by the time a man is ready to become an executive, his wife will enjoy his full-time company for two or three weeks. The way in which he chooses to spend his vacation is his personal choice, but the objective should be some change of pace and scenery in order to produce the greatest amount of mental and physical regeneration. It is for this reason that family physicians cast a jaundiced eye on the choice of too strenuous a regimen for a vacation. They are concerned with a recharging of the batteries, rather than with a total discharge of whatever energy remains. Pace yourself deliberately in whatever you choose to do in your free time.

The secret of the thoroughly good vacation is to pretend you have just resigned from the company. Either you have a well-trained group to carry on in your short absence or you don't. If you have, everything will be fine; if you have not, it's too late to worry. Make a conscious effort to drop from the surface of your mind any thoughts of your work. This is a mental discipline most managers find diffi- cult to accomplish. Their ego involvement in their job naturally leads them to assume that they are indispensable, erroneous though they know that to be. You will have to condition yourself to get the proper perspective on your relationship to your job. Your greatest asset in this connec- tion is a good sense of humor. The essentially comic qual- ity of the overly egotistical personality is universally recog- nized. The last thing you want to be is an object of derision to your people. Even worse would be to elicit their pity. These could be their reactions if they get the idea that you are afraid to take a vacation of normal length.

Because of your heavy duties and responsibilities, some careful planning will have to go into the choice of a time for you to be away. You may not find it advisable to take time off during what most people consider the normal va- cation period. This could come about quite naturally by your deferring to the wishes of your subordinates in sched- uling their vacations. In all probability their families are younger than yours, and the needs of their children are more urgent. You might discover the special charm of tak- ing an off-season vacation in a well-known spot, when ac- commodations are more plentiful and the service much more attentive and personal.

We should mention a phenomenon which occurs with fair regularity on vacations: the "great idea" which gives promise of a spectacular personal achievement for you. This serendipitous happening will actually add much to your enjoyment of your vacation. You should remember, however, that the idea probably will result from the state of relaxation you achieve. It would never have occurred during your ordinary intense concentration on the job.

To recapitulate: You should look forward to a vacation with pleasure and regard it as the dessert that follows an especially satisfying meal. When your job and your vacation are both functional, they should complement each other perfectly. Since you are so totally involved personally, it will be hard for you to assess the amount of unwinding which will occur during these periods away from work. More than likely, you will get feedback from your associates to let you know whether anything changed while you were away.

Because too much indulgence of a personal hobby such as fishing, hunting, or camping does not interrupt your routine enough to provide the full therapeutic value inherent in a well-planned vacation, most managers find it advantageous to plan a variety of vacations. The exploration of unknown places or things will often pay big dividends. You have always been resourceful as evidenced by your success on the job. Put some of that resourcefulness to work for you in getting full enjoyment from your vacations.

How Good Are Your Family Relationships?

Statistically, the chances are that you will be judged ready for an executive position at about the time your children have just left home or are preparing to do so. This is always a traumatic experience for parents, especially for the mother. Even if you still have several children at home, their situation has radically changed during the past few years while you have been a middle manager. Families often adjust to the upper-income brackets by giving their children greater mobility and autonomy.

In either event, you would do well to take stock of your family situation. There has never been a time when good relationships at home has been more important to your business career. You have enough troubles at work without complicating things by letting problems develop at home. You need strong support from your family right now.

The fact that all the members of your family with whom you still have direct contact are adult works both for and against you. We can make the assumption that, as adults, they will approach differences of opinion in the family with reason and an open mind. This ordinarily leads to smooth solutions. On the other hand, each member has his own values, and it is unlikely that they will be identical. If this gives rise to serious differences within the family circle, you may expect to have a longer and more arduous road back to a state of unity.

It is not too far out to suppose that some permanent polarizations will develop about this time in your family's growth. It is imperative that you not allow this to upset you. Concentrate on the simple fact that each member of your family has a right to opinions of his own as he approaches adulthood, and try to prevent differences from developing into family rifts. As a prospective executive, it is to be hoped that you have retained a youthful, resilient outlook on life, but it is not realistic to expect you to be as flexible as your children are when they approach adulthood. You will have to make special allowances for their feelings and convictions for several years to come—and do it gracefully.

One good result of this overall scene is that you will have many opportunities to deepen and enrich your relationship with your wife. Should she side with a dissident member of the family, you can, if you exert a little extra effort, gain much stature in the eyes of your family by working out the most practical and reasonable compromise. Work hard at this, since it will contribute mightily to the effectiveness and smoothness of your family living.

It is to be hoped that your family will be one of your more potent assets at this stage in your career. Never doubt for a moment that they will be under a discreet but searching evaluation by your associates and superiors. This has come to be standard practice in almost all companies when a new executive is being chosen, because his public image is of great importance to the success of the enterprise. This practice may be unfair, but it is a fact of life. You will be judged partially by the kind of family you have raised. To make the most of this, it is of course necessary that you communicate closely and continuously with every member of your family. This is no time for you to assume that they know what your immediate—or long-term—job objectives are. Fill them in on the background of your chances for elevation to the top echelon. Let them know what impact their actions will have on your chances for promotion, but do it without seeming to preach or be patronizing.

One of the graver dangers you face at this point is the possibility of assuming an Olympian posture in the eyes of your children. They may feel that you have become unapproachable because of the imminence of your accession to one of the more important positions in your company. The most dreaded indication of this is a drying up of spontaneity in your communications with your offspring. If anything, you should go out of your way to accentuate the fact that you are a normal, fallible human being, but one who deeply loves his family and is concerned for their welfare.

This combination of awareness and patterned activity in your home life can only have a salutary effect on your job situation. The euphoria generated by a reaffirmation of your strong familial ties will carry over to your work and will free your energy for that little bit of extra effort which you will be called upon to make so frequently from here on out. It will also enrich and magnify the feeling of accomplishment you will have when you finally succeed in achieving your goal. There is nothing like a crowd to celebrate a victory. This is a time for reassessment, reaffirmation, and recommitment, and it will be much more meaningful for you if all the members of your family have been involved in the process from the start.

Do Your People Still Like You?

Perhaps we should phrase this question in another way: How many of your people dislike you? It is not required that all your people like you in order for you to be a good manager. It is important, however, to determine whether there is any shift in your relationship with your staff. This is the ultimate test of whether job pressures are getting to you. If your anxiety level is so high that it is apparent to those who work for you, it is time for you to do something about it. Most followers have strong feelings of insecurity; their reaction to a leader who is also obviously full of tension is first fear, then dislike. It is for this reason that evidence of new enmities toward you would be significant. It may be difficult to make solid judgments as to whether this new feeling was engendered by a particular incident or whether it is a generalized reaction toward any exhibition of anxiety they have seen in you. Your concern here is only secondarily personal. Of first importance is the damage that could be done to the efficiency of your crew were this attitude to develop. At your level, it will take the disaffection of only a few people to provoke serious repercussions. And there could be no more critical time than now for your group, especially since you probably have a number of special developmental programs under way which you most assuredly do not want sabotaged.

The answer, obviously, is to keep your composure. While it is natural for your anxiety level to rise during this anticipatory time, you must make every effort to keep it from becoming apparent to your people. You cannot expect them to understand fully the reasons for your discomfort; they have grown accustomed to your strong leadership and would resent any indications that you are weakening. Most people find that the best way to control anxiety is to keep busy. A number of projects going at once constitutes the best therapy against the insidious inroads of tension. In fact, we could generalize to the extent of saying that diversionary tactics deliberately employed are nearly always effective in treating a mental attitude which is less than desirable.

We are also concerned with the state of your general

popularity right now, because a lessening of your esteem in the eyes of a few people can become an epidemic. If only one or two of your people think they have reason to change their feelings toward you, they will probably be quite vocal about discussing with their peers this major change in their working environment. This is why character assassination by innuendo and rumor is so terribly easy for one or two experts to accomplish. Of course, if you brood on this possibility you can only increase your own tensions, and this is the last thing you want to do now. You need to make a survey, but don't make too big a thing out of it, and don't dwell on any negative signals you may perceive.

Once more we face an incontrovertible fact of managerial life: that very few leaders can have both the respect and liking of all their people, and there is literally no choice between these two; respect must come first and must continue to be your personal objective in working with your crew. The natural human desire to be liked can represent a major danger to your success. You must become and remain tough-minded enough that this consideration will never interfere with the achievement of your group's goals. Better to be cordially hated by all your subordinates and make your targets than to be liked and in danger of going down the tube. As a manager of managers, you are working with people whose general outlook is much more likely to approximate objectivity than would that of a more heterogeneous group. Most of them will be well aware of the general nature of the problems facing you at this time, and they will have empathy, if not necessarily sympathy, for your position. (They may, of course, say that you have asked for whatever happens to you.)

149

It is to be hoped that this inventory of the present state of your anxiety will in itself be therapeutic. By forcing yourself to take a long hard look at the important facets of your job and how they affect your mental state, you should be able to put things into proper focus and come to the realization that, whatever happens, you are a most fortunate person. Your achievements to this point have been monumental in the eyes of most people. To everyone except a small handful, you have already arrived, and many would not be able to understand how you could be further motivated by personal ambition. Of course, this thinking is not valid for you, but knowing it exists should help to relieve, at least in small part, some of the tension you may feel while waiting for your promotion.

Whatever happens, do not let these considerations keep you from targeting in on your regular job objectives with the same vigor you have always applied. The regular routine of your work should act as a steadying influence on you. Business as usual must be your motto.

One more point: It is *not* incompatible that one part of you feel tense and anxious, while another part has peace of mind. This curious, almost schizoid state will intensify the longer you stay in management and the further up the hierarchy you climb. It is a result of the mental tradeoffs you make with yourself.

Each day that passes will bring that much nearer the resolution of your future and the final decision about your promotion. Your only personal concern is that you do everything within your control to optimize your chances. If you don't make it then, at least you will not have yourself to blame. This is of more importance to you than it might seem at this moment.

What Does Your Doctor Say?

Your doctor certainly should be speaking to you regularly these days. You owe it to yourself, your family, and the company to check regularly on the state of your health. You are now approaching the age when the degenerative diseases become a greater threat to you than they have ever been before. Moreover, increasing job pressures and longer working hours during the past few years have made you sedentary, no matter what your habits of exercise were in your youth and early adulthood.

Quite probably, your doctor will be probing deeply about the pressures under which you work. He knows better than anyone else the subtle effects that tension and anxiety can have on the human body over long periods of time. He will also be more insistent these days that some testing be done. He will want to know such things as the cholesterol level in your blood and your blood sugar level. Semiannual electrocardiograms will give him historical data on which to make a judgment as to the state of your heart.

It is curious how many people conscientiously make regular visits to the doctor—and then fail to follow his advice. It does no good to learn that you should be limiting your caloric intake in order to lose ten pounds if you refuse to do the necessary menu planning to accomplish that loss, or to let less than valid reasons keep you from taking that vigorous walk of a mile or two, or to continue buying cartons of cigarettes after what your doctor has told you about smoking and your general health.

One aspect of your relationship with your doctor is unpleasant to consider. What would you do if he were to tell you to slow your work pace, or perhaps even to take several

151

months off? Would you follow his advice, or would you rationalize your way through it and go on with the old routine? Would you level with your superior, and tell him the doctor's advice? We all find it extremely difficult to believe, deep down, in our own mortality. We tend to say, "These things will never happen to *me*." This may be true for a while yet, but are you prepared to face reality if the doctor does give you an unwelcome verdict? Far better to slow down the progress of your career than to have it come to an end.

The most important words your doctor will have for you in these years are the guidelines he gives you on maintaining your good health. He knows your hopes and aspirations almost as well as you do, and everything he tells you will be said in the light of your plans for the future. If he gives you advice you find unwelcome, you may be sure he is interested in your own ultimate good. If he finds conflict between your job situation and your future well-being, there will be only one choice in his way of thinking.

It is not our intent to dwell on the dark side of the picture. Because you have established the habit of regular physical checkups, the doctor's function will probably be simply to continue guiding you along the paths of physical fitness and avoiding a few well-known and common health hazards. Your doctor is in the curious position of being an employee of yours whose duty it is to give you orders. And you have a parallel duty to obey those orders all the way. The objective of both of you is to keep you in shape to perform on the job as well as you always have, and to prepare for the inevitably heavier stress which will be generated if you are again promoted. Your doctor certainly can help you function in the face of this pressure if you will let him.

But you will have to go along with what he says, both in spirit and in the actuality of following the steps he outlines.

Your good health is your greatest single asset.

*   *   *

It is urgent at this point that you determine how much anxiety is generated by your workload and the prospects which lie ahead for you. There are some definitive indicators which always show when your anxiety level begins to rise too high. One of them is that your sleep is likely to be disturbed. This fact in itself is disturbing and may add to the problems.

Increasing job pressures may make you more irritable than you used to be. If you find your flash point is becoming appreciably lower than it used to be, stop and take stock of your situation. High irritability can quickly sabotage the interpersonal relationships you have spent years in developing.

You should be jealous of your vacation time. Use it—for vacation. Try to be imaginative in the way you spend this time, so that new experiences can add zest to the routine of your living. The important thing is not to fail to take time away from work regularly for rest and relaxation.

This is a highly critical period in your family relationships. Take pains to communicate with the members of your family well and often. Don't assume that they know what you are thinking. They can be of help to you only when they know what your goals are and how you hope to achieve them.

If your anxiety level is too high, and it shows, you can expect a deterioration in your relationships with those who work for you. Unless you exercise great self-control, the discovery that your people don't like you as well as they used to will increase your anxiety all the more. Now is the time to demonstrate the self-control you have developed.

Finally, these are the years when guarding your health takes top priority among your activities. Listen to your doctor, and do what he says.

8

Are You a Betting Man?

THE business world, like any other, has its share of euphemisms and circumlocutions. It would be unseemly for managers to speak too freely in public of betting the company resources, especially since those are the property and capital of other people. So the terms used are "taking a calculated risk," "the management of risk," and so on. However, the simple truth is that every enterprise does a great deal of betting. As a middle manager, you have been indoctrinated into this part of your job and have learned to live with its rigors. The question now remains: Are you ready for the bigger stakes and longer odds at the executive level of the operation? The huge amounts of money involved can be overwhelming, unless you have prepared yourself well for this facet of business.

Can You Risk Your Own Assets?

Before approaching the company's side of the betting operation, however, we ask you to examine your feelings about your own assets. How freely would you be willing to put them on the block? As an executive, most of your assets, and most of those you expect to get in the future, will be inextricably bound up with the fate of the company for which you work. This means that the quality of your executive decisions will have a direct effect on the value of your own property, as well as on that of your employer. A large part of your net worth may be represented by stock in the company, either given to you as part of a deferred compensation package or made available to you at favorable prices as one of the perquisites of top management in the organization.

Of course, life itself is a gamble these days, but the man who by instinct and preference always plays it safe will never make a spectacular success of his financial life. How much of the spirit of controlled daring of your pioneering ancestors do you have? The risks you will have to take are not as apparent as theirs were, but they are just as real and will have just as far-reaching effects on your life.

The important thing, of course, is the manner in which you approach the whole subject of risk taking. The compulsive gambler chooses the longest odds available; he wants either to win it big or to be a spectacular failure. He makes little or no attempt to evaluate his chances of winning. This, obviously, is not the state you want for yourself. Your chips should be put down only after you have made every effort to learn all you can about the risks. You will have to do as much work before you take your gamble as you would for a sure thing. At some point, the available data will be exhausted, and you will then have to make a decision even though you lack some facts which could be critical to your choice of action.

The extent of your personal betting must of course depend on your reaction to the activity. Does betting a reasonable amount of your assets exhilarate you or produce unbearable tension? Can you retain your coolness and judgment under fire? When one of your major stakes seems to be directly threatened, do you panic? The answers to these questions will tell you how much of your assets you will be willing to put down on an uncertain situation.

Obviously, there is a high positive correlation between your willingness to gamble your own money and your general state of self-confidence. If you are convinced that your judgment is better than average, you will have less hesitation about backing your choices financially, and this self-confidence will increase every time you win your bet.

Another major determinant of how much gambling of a personal sort you will do is the attitude of the other members of your family. Their stake in the matter is just as real as yours. Will they be willing to stand still for the bad effects of a losing venture and undergo the drudgery of falling back and regrouping the family fortunes? More and more as they mature, your children are entitled to an explanation of the situation and of how you read the odds for success in the bets you are making.

The closer you come to the executive echelon, the more of your resources will be involved in the personal chances you take. Your ego involvement will be such that you can hardly avoid getting on the bandwagon. The more you participate in major policy making in your company, the

157

more you will be tempted to get in on the gamble and the payoff.

Can You Risk the Company's Assets?

It is one thing to put your own assets in jeopardy; it is another to take a chance with money belonging to someone else. Yet that is what you will be doing on a grand scale when you become an executive. Every new product, every major sales effort, every significant change in company policy—the things you will decide on as an executive—will be putting the enterprise's resources on the line. That is why an executive has no margin for error; if he makes one mistake, it may cripple the company.

The effect of this knowledge should be visible in your operations. You will have to be extremely careful to explore every available source of pertinent information before you make a decision. Your advisers and resource personnel will have to be as good at their jobs as you are at yours; this can be the case only if they know what the targets are.

One point should be kept constantly in mind once you are in your new position: For your calculation of the risks involved, your most valuable inputs will come to you either from your staff or from outside sources. Your direct-line subordinates are undoubtedly sharp and well informed, but their viewpoints and information are too close to yours to be helpful. Your staff people, on the other hand, have more contacts with the other functions and disciplines because of the nature of their assignments. What is more, they probably are more in touch with the outside world than are your line subordinates.

You will also be assiduously cultivating information sources among your peers and opposite numbers in other enterprises to give you the balance necessary to engender self-confidence in your decisions. You cannot continue to operate unless you have a high degree of self-confidence. The pressures would be intolerable if you thought constantly of the vast amount of wealth entrusted to your keeping, and at the same time were nagged by doubts about the quality of the calculated guesses you are called upon to make.

The assets of your company are men, money, and materials (or machinery). You will have to be prepared to bet them all, at one time or another, and sometimes all of them at once. Of the three, people are the most complex and variable. Yet, paradoxically, you will probably feel safer in your own mind about your judgments involving people than you will about those concerning money or materials. This is true because of the countless interfaces you have had with people over the years and the judgments of them which you have formed on the basis of many situations. You have come to have supreme faith in your working crew. You couldn't operate without this confidence in them, which is made greater by your awareness of both their strengths and their weaknesses and by the fact that you have often correctly predicted their reactions to a given set of circumstances.

Unless you came up through finance yourself, you are going to be more dependent on others for making decisions about your company money bets than you will about people. Modern corporate finance is an extremely esoteric art. Few people become really expert in it, and then only after a long and arduous apprenticeship. We have strongly recommended that you become an expert of sorts in economics, but acquiring real expertise in finance requires a lifetime of dedicated study. So you will be guided—up to a point—by the advice of your financial experts when you get to the money betting. The major point, however, cannot be overlooked: The final decision will be yours and yours alone.

Making your bets on company materials and machinery can be difficult, but it is the least bothersome of the three kinds of assets you are working with. The specifications and limitations of your physical properties and the machinery that makes your products are common knowledge to a large number of people, yourself included. Usually the only element of doubt here is not one of kind, but of degree. You will be concerned largely with such questions as: How far can we elasticize the maintenance schedule for ten-year-old machinery when we get into rush production runs? or, How much real flexibility do we have in existing machinery for the introduction of new product models? We certainly are not minimizing the importance of the risk taking involved in committing new facilities for new products, but, in new ventures, money and people are at least as important as projected new facilities.

You will be handsomely paid for taking these risks. In return, your management expects performance backed up by rigorous homework and your best creative thinking. You will never again be allowed the luxury of a snap decision, unless some combination of misfortunes has created the direst emergency, and this is usually the result of someone's mismanagement. We can only hope it was not yours.

The fact that you are required to play games with both

your own and the company's total resources will offer you the greatest challenge in your executive position. Compared to the total population, yours is a small, close-knit fraternity. You carry on your shoulders a significant portion of an awesome responsibility: the economic welfare of the greatest nation on earth. It would be comforting to discover some way of playing it safe so that you could always win without danger, but that's not the way the game is played. You will be forced to take chance after chance; your only real tool is the product of your thinking.

Do You Enjoy Taking a Long Chance?

If your introspection has shown you capable of risking your own belongings and your company's assets, you must answer one more question before you can be sure you are the kind of risk taker an executive must be: How long are the odds you would be willing to play? Many people find no problem in doing a little betting if they think they have a reasonable chance of winning. That is why race tracks have three kinds of tickets: win, place, and show. The cautious gambler buys a show ticket on the heavy favorite and is satisfied with a gain of only a few cents on his risk. Those who make it big in business would not buy a show ticket. Their objective is to bring home the long-odds dark horse as a winner.

It would be wrong to stretch this analogy too far, or to imply that you must be a wild gambler to be a successful executive. The executive looks for a long-odds bet to mark him as an exceptional manager. But he will first become as knowledgeable as possible in certain key areas of his gamble.

Say, for example, that he is interested in marketing a new product which is a real departure from those now available and for which a need is not widely recognized. He would undoubtedly do an extensive amount of market research to get some idea of the extent of the possible market. Through some intensive engineering design work, he would also satisfy his curiosity about the practicability of manufacturing the new product. His next concern would be the availability and costs of the necessary raw materials. If these seemed reasonably sure, he would then investigate thoroughly the amount of work which would be necessary to realign or reequip production facilities to accommodate the new product. He would hold many conferences with sales during each of these steps. Finally, he would make an in-depth study of the personnel available for transfer to the new project and would make a close estimate of the kinds of skills (and the numbers involved) necessary to get off the ground.

The collection of all these data would still leave the executive a long way from being able to make a final decision, but surely no one would call him a wild bettor if he decided to go ahead with the new project.

The general public is aware of several famous bets that failed in the business world. Two of the better known are the Teardrop Chrysler and the Edsel. In a sense, both of these were doubly tragic, since it is now obvious that the only thing wrong with their introduction was the timing. The public simply was not ready for them at the time. Both cars have been followed successfully by others which are almost their identical twins.

Timing is one of the more critical variables in the business gamble. There is no certain formula for calculating or forecasting whether the public will accept a new product or a new fashion. The executive who has two or three major successes to his credit will almost certainly have made good bets about the timing of his coups. Contrariwise, even giants can make mistakes. Sears, Roebuck and Co., by all standards the colossus of the retail merchandising field, once made an error of about 4 percent in its forecast of the next year's demand for television sets. The overproduction by the subsidiary which produced the sets, followed by heavy production cutbacks and financing necessary to store the surplus sets, caused severe dislocations in the subsidiary, so much so that nearly all the members of top management of the company found themselves in deep trouble. The fact that the trouble really was not of their making did not lessen its severity for them. The true executive must be tough minded enough to take this kind of blow and come back for more.

Of course, when you as a new executive go through one of these complex gyrations, calculate your odds, and gamble and win, the rewards will be rich indeed, both tangible and psychic. You may notice a few more gray hairs, but you will have the good feeling of knowing that you won your place among an exceedingly tough bunch of knights. It is this knowledge of the caliber and abilities of your competitors that will keep your thinking honest at all times. Their surveillance of your activities will be unremitting, and their ability to take advantage of a single gross error on your part will be painful in the extreme. You can't afford to miss.

It is obvious that this entire process would be unbearable unless you derive a purely personal pleasure from the excitement of the game. This is one of the more salient characteristics that sets you apart from others and makes you a valid candidate for top management. The reward you will value most highly from a big win lies in beating your peers to a tough objective. You probably like many of them personally, but you can't stand to see them beat you at your own game.

As a practicing executive, your job will be to see that you calculate the odds of your gambles to a degree of nicety limited only by the availability of data. Your charter says you will put large percentages of your company's assets under risk every day you work, but it also says you have the ongoing responsibility of limiting and reducing that risk by every means at your command. Your ambivalence is centered around your twin duties of being conservative with the assets entrusted to you and at the same time putting them to work for your employer under conditions of uncertainty in every venture you undertake. This is the reason for the size of that paycheck they give you, which is a source of pride and continuing amazement to you. Can you really be worth that much money to any company? You most assuredly will be if you win your long-odds bets with any degree of regularity.

How Do You Calculate the Odds?

It would be a routine matter to calculate the odds on any business risk you undertook if you were to consider only money and machines as variables. What makes the odds change is, of course, the men involved. You will, in the long run, risk both your assets and those of the company on your judgment of your competitors' ability and sharpness. You can ill afford to make a significant error in this judgment. How do you go about sizing up an individual or a group whom you may never have met and certainly know little about personally? You do it by checking the record, just as you would if you followed the horses and bet at the track.

The stakes make it eminently worth your while to spend time and effort in tracking down the salient facts about your competitors' past performance. Your assumption will always be that what shows on the surface is far from the whole truth. The most frustrating decision you can ever come to about one of your competitors is that he has been lucky a couple of times. This actually tells you nothing about his real potential or what he might be able to do under the proper stimulus. This is the man on whom you should really run a depth study before you bet against him. Since you are always taking the risk of being beaten in one of these competitions, at least assure yourself that the winner will not be a lesser man who is extending his run of luck. If you must lose, lose to the champ.

In your original search for data, follow the rules of brainstorming: Don't make a single value judgment. Accept and record every fact you can dredge up, and reserve the weighting and classifying until all the facts are in. However, make sure that you classify the data into two categories: facts and suppositions. It is easy to confuse a supposition with a hard fact, and if you do this a few times, you can assure your early retirement from the game as an injured nonhero.

Much of what you are seeking is a matter of public record, but has probably been overlooked by everyone concerned. Patent records, articles of incorporation, the annual reports of companies, legal actions, financial transactions involving the sale of stock or the floating of debentures, personnel changes—all these and other pertinent facts can be found through diligent search. The mere chronological arrangement of these data about an individual or a group can give you an idea of what has been accomplished. Help yourself visualize your competitors by actually charting out these items; you will be surprised at how much you can flesh out a concept of your rivals and how much chance you have of beating them.

These facts are valuable, but you must still isolate the personal attributes of the people concerned. How do they react to pressure? What was their response when they lost a battle? How quickly do they bounce back from adversity? Do you know any of their staff members personally, and if so, how do you rate them? Would you hire one or more of them if you were given the opportunity? Do either the principals or any of their staff members have a reputation for being authorities in their field?

If you are really interested in winning a bet with one of these adversaries, you will have a consuming curiosity about their possible weaknesses. Is there a blind side in their makeup? What is it? How do you propose to approach it? In following this problem, be sure your rival doesn't surprise you first and beat you before you can get off the ground.

The one possibility of rigging the odds in your favor is to make a bet with a man without his knowledge. On extremely rare occasions you can launch a new product or service and completely surprise your competition. Be sure you make the payoff from that happy event a big one, because the odds against its happening to you again are fantastically high.

You must also take considerable pains to cover your tracks. Learn and cultivate the use of the feint and the red herring. The only trail you leave visible should be a false one. Because of the continuing necessity for team effort in all your major undertakings, this defensive action is very difficult. When more than one person is involved, true secrecy about operations requires assorted miracles. That is why speed in decision making and implementation is of such paramount importance when taking business risks.

The key to success here is to take all the time necessary to gather pertinent data, sort it out, and judge the importance of each item. But, once you have done this and have decided to go on with the game, put yourself and your entire organization into high gear, and concentrate relentlessly on winning. From here on out, you can afford no interruption until the results of the action are in.

Keep in mind that there is only one underlying purpose to all this furious activity: to give you a chance to calculate the odds of the bet you are making with a reasonable degree of accuracy. This is not the final go/no-go decision; that will still have to be made after you have satisfied your questions about the odds you will have to play if you do decide to go.

It is neither desirable nor necessary that you keep your own counsel about all this activity. You have one or more persons to whom you report, and they will not take it kindly if you make these major decisions on a purely unilateral basis. One of the main premises on which your executive appointment will be made is that your supervisors have greater expertise and more experience than you do. Get their advice before you make your decision.

When Is the Bet Worthwhile for You?

No matter how ready you may be to risk your own and the company's assets, no matter how much you may enjoy taking a long chance or how well you can calculate the odds, you must have a feeling of rightness about the matter. This intuitive feeling, however, does have some identifiable parts. First, your opponent is worthy of your steel. Almost any executive will shy away from taking on a competitor who is clearly his inferior. Oddly enough, the real executive tends not to recognize the opposite situation when he himself is clearly the underdog. His ego may not let him admit this unless he clearly takes a beating, and even then he is likely to offer some rationalizations for having lost.

Second, glamour is inherent in the setup. A bet for dollars alone is not highly attractive to a majority of executives. Actually, the objective itself must have an interest and drawing power in order to get their commitment. One of the most attractive lures is the local fame (in the enterprise or in the industry) which will be theirs for winning at long odds. Executives are highly motivated by the prospects of esteem and good reputation among their peers and subordinates. If the odds are too long against them, they will probably shy away from the bet.

You will not be successful over the long haul as an executive if you are a compulsive gambler; there must be a reasonable chance for winning, even if remote. Moreover, you will inevitably demand that your working team be adequate and prepared to carry the extra load which will be imposed upon them during the run for the laurel. You think too much of your people to throw them to the lions in an obviously losing cause. Granted, they will have to be prepared to lose, but only after having had a fighting chance to win.

One of the more important prerequisites for entering the contest is that you have free rein and full control of your efforts. This must be a clearly stated element of your position description: autonomy to make your decisions and then to act under your own direction when taking your risks. If you have the slightest feeling that you are a marionette, you will find the situation intolerable and will refuse the bet. In fact, you will doubtless carry this one step further and demand the full cooperation of those to whom you report throughout the contest. Of course, limits and ground rules will have been established before you took on the contest, but within those constraints you will need the full efforts of everyone in your organization. You are actually demanding a full complement of tools to do the job. Moreover, the tools must be first-rate and kept in perfect repair. You are as much a craftsman in your field as the master mechanic is in his.

If you are like most executives, you will also want resource people with whom you can counsel at every step of the way. Ordinarily, they will not be within your organization. You will turn more naturally to peers or friends in other businesses in order to get a sounding about your tactics and their probable results. Typically, you will call upon these people from the very beginning and throughout the action. You may or may not change your decisions as a result of their advice, but you will feel better for having unburdened yourself to someone. Many executives use a psychiatrist for this purpose, since they know he is pledged to secrecy. Also, large numbers of highly placed businessmen regularly consult astrologers; this will seem less weird when you realize that most betting people are highly superstitious in one or several ways. They insist that the signs be right before they undertake a major venture, and perhaps this is just as well, since such beliefs function as a safety valve for their highly emotional state during the race.

We have listed several conditions which most executives demand before taking on a major risk, but these do not add up to the final decision. There still remains that indefinable element of intuition, which is critical. If the decision were based purely on the other conditions, most of the risk and all the excitement of the chase would be removed. The attractive bet will demand every ounce of your concentration, every particle of your mental and emotional resources during the action. Nothing less than this full commitment could make the risk worthwhile. Unless you are totally involved, the effort will not pay off.

Obviously, your development as an executive will be geared to an increased scope and difficulty of the risks you undertake. Certainly, you would not be satisfied with a declining level of action as you proceed. The escalation of effort must not be too swift, but it must be there on a continuing basis. The outcome of this graded series will naturally be growth and prosperity for your organization and for yourself.

Are You a Winner?

We have left the most important criterion of risk taking for the last. If you have put all the other elements together correctly, you will have a better than even chance of winning your bet. The biggest question then becomes: Are you a winner?

The anatomy of losing has always been studied, but scant attention has been paid to the protocol of winning well and gracefully. If the results of the first two or three significant risks you assume are favorable, your success could easily lead you to conclude that your executive position is not so difficult as it has been advertised to be and that you are obviously by nature and training admirably suited to your job and need not worry about your future. This attitude is, of course, the natural breeding ground for a terrific letdown. The carelessness engendered by this attitude can be fatal to your chances of winning your next big bet. Somewhere along the line, you will cut a corner, or fail to obtain all the necessary data, and your decision will be wrong.

The superiority complex born of a quick success or two is also sure to affect your interpersonal relationships. Both peers and subordinates will notice a new hauteur in your bearing which can be irritating and abrasive. You attitude will also be reflected in your new habits of making snap judgments and ruthlessly cutting off the arguments of anyone who disagrees with you. The result of these changes in you will be an immediate cessation of the natural flow of communication you have spent years in building up. You must avoid falling into the trap of assumed omniscience and invulnerability. This is going to take some of the most rigorous self-discipline you have ever exercised. If you feel strongly against asking for direct readings about your personality from your subordinates, you might consider asking a staff specialist, such as the company's industrial psychologist, to run periodic informal surveys of your people's attitudes toward you. Then again, your own perception should tell you almost immediately if there is a significant lessening of incoming communications. The resignation of a single staff member without a valid reason is almost certainly a red flag.

We are not belittling the euphoria which will naturally follow when you win after taking a big risk. This gives you the mental and spiritual impetus which will be reflected in increased creativity. You will not want to do anything to interfere with this cycle. But, while you are using this flow of extra energy, you should also be giving extra attention to maintaining a brake on your ego. With every big risk for which you engineer a winning effort, you will grow and develop as an executive. This growth must be natural and solid, rather than an insubstantial mushroom. Herein lies one of the gross differences in degree which distinguish the executive from the middle manager. The adjustment is a subtle one and will demand sensitivity and perceptivity.

One factor which tends to blur clear vision of this problem of ego growth is the long time which ordinarily elapses between your decision making and the final evaluation of its quality. How much have outside independent variables muddied the waters and made clean judgment of your decision extremely difficult? Above all else, you must avoid taking refuge in these external variables to rationalize a partial or total failure in a risk situation. You, if no one else, will without doubt know whether your decision was faulty or whether you were blown out of the water by a torpedo from an unseen submarine. Of course, we are assuming that you will win nearly all your bets and will live to retire as an honored elder statesman.

*　　*　　*

So much of your activity as an executive is bound up in a risk-taking environment that this must be considered as a discrete segment of your work. Because your personal fortunes are tied to the company's, you must be willing to risk your own assets. After that, you must have the self-confidence and poise to be willing to risk, in some cases, the entire success of your enterprise. Moreover, you must do this without letting your anxiety level rise to the point where it will interfere with clear thinking and decision making.

You must get some enjoyment from taking a long chance, if for no other reason than savoring the big rewards which will be yours when you win. Before you accept the long chance, you must establish a routine for pinpointing the odds you are facing. There are ways open to you for minimizing the negative aspects of the risk.

From the standpoint of your personal expectations, the assumption of the risk must be worthwhile to you. The game itself must have a fascination for you, or the associated trauma would be too much to bear. Finally, one of the sterner processes of your self-development as an executive lies in conditioning yourself to be a good winner. Your continued success, both in interpersonal relationships and in your actual job, is closely interwoven with this ability.

9

What's Your Game Plan?

TEAM athletes in competitive sports such as football and basketball must follow carefully thought-out plans in order to win. The team captain is responsible for overseeing and directing the action in accordance with the plan. You are the playing captain of a team engaged in one of the most fiercely competitive situations in the world. At this particular juncture, your objective is purely personal: promotion to the executive echelon of the enterprise for which you work. To attain it, you are going to have to involve the members of your working organization in many ways, since you are measured by *their* accomplishments, rather than by your personal work output.

Do You Really Know Your Goal?

It now becomes urgent that you know exactly what your goals are for each step of the way toward your overall objective of promotion. You cannot announce to the general public that you are absorbed in satisfying a personal and selfish goal. Your overt signals must be totally centered on achieving your organizational objectives as quickly and economically as possible. This is why, from here on in, your game plan will make or break your career. Every decision, every action, every move you make with your group must fit exactly into a mosaic which, when completed, will constitute your big design.

Everything you have done before now during your time in management has in effect been concerned with acquiring and sharpening the tools you will now use. Your human, technical, and conceptual skills must be functional both individually and as a perfectly blended network to help you get your work done. Essentially, your immediate objective in the actions you undertake must be to increase the luster of your image with those to whom you report. Self-serving and cold blooded though this may sound, it is the pure and simple truth. You have no time left for excursions down attractive byways; your rivals are pounding down the main trail. Because the number of candidates for the executive echelon is small, each is subjected to intensive scrutiny. Every action you take, every decision you make will be under the glass until it has been thoroughly evaluated and judged. Thus, right now the planning function of your management job assumes an importance far greater than it ever had before, and this will go on until the time of decision about your promotion.

Before implementing your plans, you must subject them to all logical, financial, and personnel arguments. This is especially true of any innovations you have in mind, and of course you do want to have a number of successful ones on your record. These truly separate the pro from the amateur.

One of the more important reasons for doing intensive planning at this stage of the game is your own peace of mind. Your anxiety level will be high enough without leaving a blank in your activity which will cause it to escalate still further. It will reassure you greatly to know that every possible contingency has been prepared for and that you will not be taken by surprise by unforeseen events. Your mentors will be watching to see how poised you are under this unremitting pressure. You must be unflappable.

In asking you whether you really know what your goal is, we are assuming that your desire for the executive position is unshakable. At this point, what has motivated you to want the job is not important; we are concerned only with the best way of getting you there. However, the matter of your motivation will continue to be of supreme importance to you, inasmuch as it will govern the actions you take toward your goal. Does this job represent to you power, status, money, influence, a chance for personal growth and self-actualization, or a combination of some or all of these motivators? Remember, that whatever your personal goal is, it cannot diverge from the objectives of your enterprise. Unless they are in consonance, you haven't a ghost of a chance for final success. No one man can be as big as the enterprise; each has to fit himself to it.

There is another sobering thought: From this point forward, the achievement of your goals will have a visible effect on the course of the company, since you will be working with the whole corporate being in your decisions and actions. Therefore, you must visualize completely and accurately the probable effects of whatever course you take. And once again, this brings us face to face with the ultimate responsibility of managers at any level: the best for the most. Certainly, you cannot now afford to make any decision or take any action that will benefit a few and possibly be detrimental to many. This would be self-defeating and fatal to your chances for making it at the top level. However, this managerial duty is in itself a handy tool for measuring your plans. Using that responsibility as your frame of reference will make many of your decisions quite simple and clear-cut. If your proposed action will benefit the entire organization, go; if not, forget it. It's as simple as that. The natural corollary is that when the enterprise is bettered, so is your own situation.

Rarely will your original game plan proceed to completion without some alterations, either minor or major. Therefore, your planning activity should be continuous throughout the action. Daily reviews of it must be routine. The whole point is that you must be on top of it.

What's Your Next Move?

An agonizing time of waiting occurs between your arrival at readiness for promotion and the appearance of a vacancy. Even your involvement with the countless details of your present job does not shorten the time for you, because you realize how relatively brief the remainder of your working career will be, and there are so many things you want to accomplish. The pressure on you builds nearly to the bursting point, but what can you do? If you make overt motions toward those responsible for choosing the next executive, there is the strong possibility that they may downgrade you for doing so. On the other hand, if you give the appearance of not caring what happens, they may question how much you want to be advanced. You are caught on the horns of a dilemma.

The shadings of this situation are delicate in the extreme, and it will take every ounce of your sensitivity to walk this path. The cues you do receive will be all but invisible and inaudible; you will have to make some split-second decisions about whether to take action or to remain quiet and wait.

There is one particularly dangerous ploy which has been used successfully a few times by executive candidates who felt hopelessly boxed in while waiting for promotion. That ploy is to be seen once or twice in the company of a member of an executive search organization. Just how you are going to arrange this without actually putting yourself on the auction block is your problem—unless you are not averse to having them look around for you. Of course, in reality executive searchers never let the candidate know he is under consideration until there is an 80 percent or better chance that he will be the one picked by the client; so, if you elect to use this ploy, it will be an innocent action for both you and the searcher. The danger in using it at all is obvious. If the word gets back to those in charge that you are restive, they may decide that your staying power isn't sufficient for the demands of the job they have in mind for you, and you may undo the careful work of years.

But it may be just as dangerous to freeze in your tracks and do nothing. Accustomed as you are to action, doing nothing certainly will be harder on you, and your mentors could read this as a sign that your initiative is waning. They may make cryptic comments among themselves about your peaking out at an unseemly early age and wonder where your drive has gone.

The one thing about this situation you can be sure of is that there is no formula for successful strategy. Each case is unique. You will have to study and evaluate every factor of the environment within which you are operating. The situation will make or break you on the basis of the accuracy with which you predict the reactions of the principals. You have been gathering the background for these predictions during all the years you have worked with them, and you have before now frequently succeeded in guessing which way they would jump. If, as is usual, several of these men are concerned with selecting new executives, you will have to decide for yourself which of them will have the most to say, and be guided in your own actions by your estimate of his thinking. That is, there might be several in the group who would react negatively if you were to make an obvious move to attract attention to yourself. But, if the most important member of the group would think of this move in positive terms, you would probably decide to go ahead. The fact that this whole picture is so tenuous and hard to read is in itself a close simulation of what your whole working life will be like after you are promoted. It is because of this that executives are hard to find and are well paid once discovered. If executive decisions came easily, they could be bought cheaply.

Actually, this predicament is a preview of the isolation you will be operating in as an executive. You will probably hesitate at this point even to take your immediate superior into your confidence about your feelings. This is especially true if he will have a major voice in deciding whether you are to be promoted. This is not to say that you will, or should, suddenly withdraw and refuse to communicate any more with your boss. But there will be some sensitive areas in your relationship with him which were not apparent before. What is more, he will probably be aware of this and be sympathetic toward your position.

The one point which should be strongly reinforced is that you must not allow this never-never land to sap you of your decision-making ability at this crucial time. It is more urgent now than ever before that you do make a move when you are convinced that the scene is set. Some of the chips may be big ones, but you must still let them fall where they may. This is the time in your life to adopt a fatalistic attitude. It is about the only protection you can find for the exposure of your position and your resultant vulnerability. What is to be will be. You have prepared yourself to the utmost of your ability to assume greater responsibility. Your development program has had careful and expert design, and you have pursued it rigorously. Your work situation itself has been the best prep school you could have picked for what lies ahead, and you have been a star pupil. In a real sense, things are now out of your hands, so why worry?

One of the things you can do to double-check your position is to pay especial attention to the cues your subordinates are giving you. Their interest in what is going on is extremely keen, for their futures are much involved. It is entirely possible that their perception of what is going on is clearer than your own, so why not check their observations and impressions? We are assuming, of course, that your relationship with them will allow you to do this without upsetting yourself or them. You could do much worse than listen to their ideas and ask their counsel before making up your own mind about your next move. If you have chosen your people well, they should be valuable to you at this time.

When we strip the situation of all inconsequential things, it is apparent that your only real ally now is whatever patience you can muster to carry you over the waiting period. You must depend on your own resources.

To Whom Have You Talked About Your Plans?

Your choice of confidants takes on added importance at this turning point in your career. Every personal decision you make right now is a crucial one, and the quality of the advice you seek and get will have an enormous influence on the rest of your life. One of the first things you should do is to take a good hard look at those to whom you have been going for counsel up to now. Your situation is changing significantly, but is theirs? In other words, are you moving so far apart that their perceptions will no longer be valid for your position? For example, the planning you are now doing has a longer time span; will your old friends' judgments have the same validity they had when you were a middle manager? You need sharp, clear, and correct answers to these questions.

One thing has not changed: You will still be expected to turn to your boss for the formal aspects of your development program, just as you always have. He has a vested interest in its success, and every right to be kept abreast of your progress. (It goes without saying that you still owe him the routine communication about the job you are doing. He cannot be expected to operate in a vacuum, any more than you would.) But this does not mean that you will necessarily bare your soul to him concerning every last detail of your campaign for advancement. This is especially true if you know that he does not have complete autonomy about your promotion, and it is unlikely that he does. It is now mandatory that you begin to operate as an individual, especially in this area. You may have to observe the forms because it is expected of you, but you may withhold from him the essence of your actions leading toward an executive appointment, at least for the present. If he is as alert as he should be, he will recognize what is going on; if he is of true executive caliber, he will respect your right to keep your own counsel at this juncture.

Now is probably the time when you will start to count heavily on the inputs of friends and colleagues outside your own organization. They have no ax to grind and will be as nearly neutral and objective in their judgments as human beings can be. Their possible lack of intimate knowledge of your enterprise will be more than overcome by their general expertise in your field and by their broad knowledge of management as a science and an art. Though you should now begin to operate as an individual, you should be capable of seeking help elsewhere and building it into your final decisions. Your ability to recognize your need for outside assistance, and to obtain it, is a sure sign of mental and emotional maturity. It is the insecure person who insists on blustering his way through without help.

Most certainly, this is the time when you should also

seek the personal assistance of any of your own company executives who have shown an interest in you. If you approach them properly, there will be no question of your seeking special favor; it is part of their job to give guidance to a subordinate who is trying to get ahead. Psychologically, the more of them you can involve in your development, the better your chances for promotion when a vacancy occurs. It is to be hoped that they would not vote for you purely on the basis of personal friendship, but any normal person tends to favor a candidate he knows and understands.

What we have just described differs in a fundamental sense from playing politics, in which case you are openly using personal influence. In contrast, you are in effect asking the executives to vote for the best man and hoping they will recognize you as that person. And that, finally, is the best political gambit there is, as any often-reelected public official could tell you.

You may decide not to confide your entire game plan to any one person. To do so can have the effect of making you vulnerable and leaving you exposed. Of course, if your various confidants communicate enough among themselves, they can eventually piece together your master strategy, but if they do they will respect you the more for not having tipped your hand to any one person.

All this is fine training for your regular job situation when you become an executive. You will then have to adopt this method as a way of life; seldom will you be able to risk laying out the entire pattern of your plans to someone at your own level or below. Only your bosses will have a right to know the entire picture, and there are times when they might respect your reticence.

In spite of all we have said, and in spite of all your elaborate planning and development, the change you are about to make is not as great as the one you underwent when you first became a supervisor. What you are going through now is more in the nature of a shift in emphasis, along with a lengthening of the time increments involved. But you will not be required to go through a total mental reorientation such as you did when you first entered management. Your commitment now is more cluttered with your personal assets, but it should not be essentially any greater than it was on your first day as a supervisor. You have been called upon to develop and hone your conceptual skills in anticipation of your next move, but you have lost little of your need for human skills. Those will be employed in interaction with fewer people, but their importance to your success has not lessened one iota. Your technical skills have long since been submerged; you are obsolescent, if not obsolete, in your original field of knowledge. For several years you have been hiring the technical skills of the newest crop of bright young graduates. This is as it should be.

Do You Have a Timetable?

You have been living with timetables ever since you entered management. Your planning is done in terms of time increments. It would be foolish not to devise a timetable for your personal development and gear it to your best estimate of the timing of certain probable executive vacancies. Although there is a fable that executives' ages are classified information, in reality they are a matter of common knowledge to close associates. This, in light of your enterprise's retirement policy, gives you an automatic timetable. Of course, no one can predict the sudden deaths, terminations, and early retirements which will take place in the executive ranks. If your company is large enough, actuaries can give you a statistically sound estimate of the numbers of these events which will occur over a five- or ten-year period. But statistical projections can be applied only to very large groups; they cannot help you guess which individuals might be involved.

Your best bet is obviously to make a compromise between the known dates of mandatory retirement and some of the other imponderables just mentioned. Your aim should be to prepare yourself well in advance of a given set point on your master timetable and to be sure that you are then ready for promotion. The items you choose to build into your development program will strongly influence the time involved in their accomplishment. For example, if you feel it urgent that you be ready within two years, you would be ill-advised to lay out a master plan for development which could not be completed in less than three years. On the other hand, the constraints put on you by the actual timetable will restrict the items you choose to work on. These diametrically opposite viewpoints of your timetable must be reconciled in the actual practice and direction of your development.

If it is your intention to take on any more projects which will remove you from the job for a period of weeks or months, you should plan these so that you will be back at work for an extended time before any anticipated possibility of promotion. This is recommended as much for your peace of mind as for any other reason. Most of us vigorously dislike the sensation of being hurried into a new job. Although the stream of events may move quite quickly, we need the illusion of a leisurely approach to a new environment. And the executive appointment will be new, even if the physical setting and the people around you do not change. The timetable you devise should extend well beyond the anticipated time of your promotion to give you a chance to orient yourself mentally to the change in your work content.

One other thing should be remembered: Your people will be undergoing a readjustment more upsetting to them than your own is to you. In their eyes, you will have changed into an entirely different person. There is nothing you can really do to prevent this from happening, but you can, with sensitivity, lessen the intensity of their trauma.

Another point you should consider is that your promotion will leave a gaping hole in your present organization. One of the most dangerous temptations facing you during this period of transition is that of attempting to mold your replacement into a carbon copy of yourself. It is mandatory that you allow him to have a personality and a managerial style of his own. There will be noticeable changes in your crew as he establishes himself, even if there are no resignations. This is the way it should be. You demanded the same consideration every time you took over a new job in management, and you owe your successor the same courtesy.

Your timetable must be large enough and flexible enough to take care of some ancillary considerations. When you become an executive, your social life will expand to include a number of new people. Your family situation will change as your wife and children feel the repercussions of your advancement. Demands will be made on them which they are not used to, and you may have to devote considerable time and attention to reducing their problems. To use a homely example, if the son of a middle manager were given a traffic ticket, this would cause few ripples on the local scene. If the same thing happened to the son of an executive, the event could easily make headlines in the local press. You have every right to assume that your wife, as a mature adult, will adjust to your change more easily than will your children, but don't be shocked if such is not the case. This is one of the many times when she will need an extra portion of tender loving care.

You could be pardoned for becoming quite frustrated at the need to draw up a timetable for events over which you have so little real control. Your success will be strictly limited by your versatility and your imagination. Once more, you should plan for every conceivable contingency, wild and improbable though some of them may seem. The important thing is not to be unprepared for any eventuality. Neither should you be downcast if some of the alternatives you choose don't prove viable when put to the test. What you are after here is a high batting average; if you win significantly more than you lose, you are on the right track.

One of the best results of this timetable activity will be the reduction of your anxiety and feeling of pressure. Just the fact that you are active and hard at work will lower the tension under which you operate. Also, your pain threshold will actually be raised if you practice the preventive therapy of adopting a fatalistic attitude. You will have done everything that could be expected of you.

How Many Time-Outs Do You Have Left?

The athlete in games like football and basketball, which are played against measured time, can call for time-outs; that is, he can bring the action to a halt so that he can rest or, what is more common, so that he can review his game plan with the other players or with the coach. It is quite probable that once or several times since you have been in management, your situation approximated a time-out. If you ever attended a long seminar (a month or more, or perhaps even a semester at a college) as part of your development program, you were completely cut off from the old familiar business of your enterprise. You did this so that you could concentrate fully on your new training effort, without the intrusions and distractions which would be routine on the job. You benefited from the seminar; moreover, you probably came back to the job with renewed vigor and zest.

Your available time for this sort of luxury is very nearly over. The tempo will quicken from here on out, and your competition will keep unremitting pressure on you until the big choice is made. You might consider going away for one more major seminar before your promotion, but you should check this out thoroughly with your superiors before you do. If there is one dissenting opinion, you would do better to remain at the scene of the action. You are not indispensable to the company, but your presence may be indispensable to your chances of being promoted. The absent candidate can be forgotten in a matter of days, and propinquity unfortunately still has a great deal to do with choosing the new executive.

This does not mean that you cannot take an occasional break. The way to do it is to change your method of operation and take much more frequent time-outs of lesser duration. An hour or two can be extremely refreshing if you use it properly. As an executive, you will have built-in access to privacy in the design of your office suite. Moreover, your people will quickly become accustomed to your disappearing frequently during the business day. So, as you can contrive it, take a couple of hours away from the job right in your office. The mental discipline involved is no small matter. It will be difficult at first to turn your mind completely away from job matters while staying in your office, but if you can learn to do it, the habit will be invaluable to you. Do some of that reading you have been promising yourself for years, but confine yourself to reading in a field entirely different from your business. Write a little. Whether you realize it or not, you are becoming a figure to command the respect of many people. They will listen to what you have to say in your area of expertise, as will others you don't yet know. Get a couple of articles written and published during these time-outs. Your associates and your bosses will gain a new measure of your worth to the enterprise from this activity.

With the amount of discretionary time you will now have at your command, you will not find it too difficult to engineer an absence of a half day every week or so. Maybe you will find the best recuperation on the golf course, or taking your wife to lunch and spending the afternoon shopping for things she would love to have you buy for her, or getting reacquainted with your grown children or your grandchildren. Of course, you are eminently capable

189

of thinking up the best ways to utilize the time. The important thing is that you establish the habit of carving this time out of your schedule on a more or less regular basis.

You will need some accomplices in this activity. The cooperation of your secretary is a must, because she has to know where to find you if there is a real emergency. You are being paid for your 24-hour availability to the job. Your key subordinates can often help by making some small decisions for you when you are away. You do want to help them develop on the job, don't you? If properly organized, this benign little conspiracy can be made to work for the benefit of many people.

One of the most pleasant results of your time-outs will be the better frame of mind you will enjoy when you are on the firing line. You will be able to face your problems with renewed energy and sharpened intellect when you return from these odd moments of recreation. The master violinist always eases the tension on the strings of his instrument when it is not in use. Nothing can pay you for taking on the onerous tasks of your executive position unless you get real personal enjoyment from the overall job.

It is obvious from what we have been saying that you will have an infinite number of time-outs left if you order your future in this manner. If you have a real right to be an executive, you must have the personal strength of will to control these small bits of your life. This is one way in which you can use the isolation inherent in your job and make it work for your good and that of the enterprise. In all probability, you will derive personal pleasure from using some of these times apart to do your conceptualizing. Actually, parts of your job come under the heading of recreation.

Does Your Coach Let You Run Your Own Game?

There are two major reasons why your boss might practice delegation on a string. First, he may be a perfectionist who feels that there is no one else capable of doing a job as well as he can. If he is fascinated and frustrated by the infinity of details he has to take care of personally, he gets little accomplished. Neither do you. He won't let you, although he probably mouths double-talk and bafflegab about the sanctity of delegation and the complete autonomy his subordinates enjoy. Unfortunately, he has probably conned himself into believing this, and would be terribly hurt if anyone were to confront him with the truth. Perfectionists may be found anywhere in management; wherever they are, they are miscast. The only effective development you can achieve in this climate is what your ingenuity can contrive without his knowledge, or while you are off the job. He would feel deeply threatened to see you growing significantly as a manager. Of course, any growth you could gain under his domination would be especially noticeable to the real executives of the enterprise. It may be that the best action for your future would be to ask for a transfer.

A second reason why your boss might not let you call the shots in your own game is nearly as unfortunate: He sincerely believes that you aren't capable of doing it. If he is correct, you have no right to be considered a candidate for an executive position. If his judgment is faulty, and the result of his own misperception, you have a tough job making him see the light. Your performance must be better than otherwise required to force him to acknowledge your readiness for promotion. The failure to achieve rapport may result from your having different values. He may be a great man for planning, while you tend to emphasize matters of organization. Or perhaps you have widely differing managerial styles. He may be strongly task-oriented, while you tend to be more people-oriented. If these differences exist, you may be too far apart philosophically to have a good working relationship.

If your boss has a strong paternal feeling for you, he may behave like a parent who cannot visualize his child as an adult. In such circumstances, you will probably be able to appeal to your boss's essential fairness and sound reasoning if you give him a little time and a good hard sell.

If you have difficulty getting autonomy in your regular job activities, there is always the special project to fall back on. Formulate an idea for one, then make a real production of it all the way. Be sure that complete documentation of every step is sent to the responsible parties, then press them for feedback if at all feasible. And whatever you do, pick a project that is quantifiable and measurable in hard dollars. This is no time for blue-sky activities. Proven executives can afford the altruistic gesture; the candidate for the job must be a pragmatist.

In any event, you will have to contrive some way to get control of your operations for a considerable period of time before you can expect to be promoted. Those responsible are not measuring your boss; they are looking at you. They want to know what you can do when you have the ball as well as the direction of the team.

Essentially, you have completed your campaign for your dream haven. Little more will affect the balance when the accounts are finally cast up. It is to be hoped that you will be judged fairly, accurately, and completely on both your record and your potential for further growth and development. You have already made some great contributions to your enterprise, but your best times lie ahead of you.

*   *   *

This chapter has been a calculated attempt to force you to crystallize your final plans for the attack on the executive suite. You must redetermine and reevaluate your personal goals to be sure that you are shooting at the right target. To hit the bull's-eye, your sights must be recalibrated for drift and windage.

At this point, the choice of your next move is a crucial determinant of your final success or failure. It will call for your best judgment and discrimination. Often, the hardest choice of all is to make no overt move, but to wait calmly for things to be resolved.

It is of the utmost importance that you go to the right people for your personal counseling. In all probability, these people will be outside your own group of associates. You need the advice of someone whose objectivity is clear and unclouded if it is to be of real value to you.

You must make a timetable, and it must extend beyond your appointment to an executive position. The transition into the new job is too critical to be left to chance. Part of your readjustment will be concerned with finding a formula for your time-outs; you must have repeated breaks from work to release pressure and to fall back and regroup. It is fortunate that you will have more discretionary time at your command than you ever enjoyed as a manager.

Most important of all is to find a way to insure that you have control of the situation for the last few months before the decision is made about your promotion. You must be able to present uncontaminated data to those responsible for picking executives. Your record must be clearly delineated in order for it to be fairly judged.

10

Can You Stay There
If You Get There?

No matter how long you have been in middle management, no matter how many contacts you have had with the executive echelon, no matter how much effort your immediate boss has made to show you what it is like on mahogany row, you will never really understand what life there is like until you have lived it. The exposure you have had has been too brief and is unquestionably distorted toward the good side or the bad; it has not provided an accurate picture of what to expect after your promotion.

In these pages we have listed many of the points of difference you may expect to find between your present job and that of the executive, and we have emphasized that many of these are differences in degree rather than in kind. But it is almost impossible to forecast with any real accuracy how anyone will react to this important promotion.

Your principal concern is, of course, whether you will respond well or badly to the twin demons of job pressure and isolation. These are the psyche warpers with which the executive has to contend for the rest of his career. It is noteworthy, but not particularly helpful, that few people in the organization can exert pressure on the executive and that most of the pressure on him is self-generated, arising from his own commitment and dedication to the good of the enterprise and his knowledge of how many other people are dependent on his good judgment for their future welfare.

You will experience great ambivalence about the isolation of the executive. In certain cases, of course, it will be extremely functional, as for example when you need total concentration before making a decision. Yet a large part of your energy will be devoted to reducing that isolation in order to assure yourself that your communications network is functional and adequate.

Most men find unpleasant another attribute of the executive position: their elevation to the status of a demigod by everyone around them. It takes great strength of character to keep one's perspective in the face of flattery and obsequiousness. However, true leaders exhibit the native power to combat such nagging problems and emerge serene and confident.

It would indeed be tragic if you were to spend half your working life preparing yourself for this step, only to learn that your goal, once achieved, was distasteful to you. You would do well to consider the alternatives open to you if this should be the case. First, you could grit your teeth and carry on, knowing that the rest of your working life would not be pleasant and that all the zest would be gone. You might be forced to choose this stoic reaction if you have been putting all your eggs in one economic basket for some years past. Second, you could quietly but urgently look for another middle management job in another enterprise, resign from your new executive position, and go back to doing work that you find comfortable. To most people, this choice would have the flavor of defeat, although it could prolong your life. Third—and there are increasing numbers of men who are choosing this alternative—you could resign your position and set yourself up as a consultant to management, with a fair prospect of making more than a comfortable living for as long as you are able to work. Actually, you would be anticipating by only a few years a common action of retired executives. In this busy and expanding business world of ours, there are many uses for the expertise and judgment you have acquired throughout your long apprenticeship.

But enough of this dirge. Chances are that you will be enchanted by your new position and will find new channels for your natural talents and acquired abilities. Your major concern will be whether you can maintain the position of eminence you have so laboriously acquired. You will be the target, today and every day, for those who are jealous of your success. Even your own boss may be waiting in ambush. Try that thought on for size, and ask yourself how you would react to that situation. The thin atmosphere you will be living in as an executive magnifies threats as well as everything else. And the better your performance, the greater the threat you may pose to your boss or to others.

The best thing to do is to approach your promotion with as little tension as possible and to assess the situation thoroughly before you allow yourself to exhibit any emotion about it. Remember that you have directed your thinking and your actions toward this goal. Your assumption all along has been that this is what you want and that you will find supreme self-satisfaction in being allowed to operate at this level for the remainder of your career. You have already conceptualized many projects for yourself; you have many plans for enlarging the scope, reputation, and profits of the enterprise in which you have involved yourself so completely. So go to it.

The finest asset you now have is the impetus you have generated in the approach to your objective. Some of the projects you initiated in your campaign still have not come to fruition; you can expect dividends from them long after you are in your new situation. Play this to the hilt, and dovetail these projects with the plans you have evolved for your executive action. Make your own luck.

How Good Is Your Sense of Balance?

Much of your activity as an executive will require good coordination and a superior sense of balance. There will be forces working on you from all directions and with varying degrees of intensity. What do you do when someone urges you to take an action which you feel in your bones is self-serving for him, yet appears on the surface to be in the best interests of the company? How do you reconcile apparent conflicts between the overall objectives of the enterprise and the economic safety of a significant number of your employees? What will be your position on pervasive environmental problems? How far do you go in fighting it out with the community if an effluent from your plant is polluting a local trout stream, but keeping the waters clean would be extremely expensive to your operations? How much do you get mixed up in local or state politics to forestall the imposition of new taxes on industry when one of the parties advocates such a course? And, speaking of politics, where are you going to align yourself in the company managerial infighting?

These are only a few of the problems for which you will have to come up with workable solutions quickly and definitively once you become an executive. There is no side-stepping them; they will confront you squarely and demand to be resolved. It is imperative, therefore, that you cultivate a sure instinct for putting the various elements of these problems into perspective and arriving at a proper balance in settling them. What is the best for the most? This approach, however, can lead to simplistic solutions unless you are extremely careful. Seldom will a superficial analysis guarantee that you have satisfied the demands of that question; an in-depth study is a must for any problem demanding an executive decision.

Of course, if you allow your subordinates to hand on to you problems which they should be answering, you are in big trouble. The fascination of the power you hold must not be allowed to cloud your vision of the overall functioning of your organization. A large part of the power inherent in your job is based on the contributions of your subordinates as they do what is rightfully their work.

To maintain a proper sense of balance is going to demand that you give some attention to the division of your labor among the various elements of your job. It would be easier at this point to dwell on your favorite work areas more than ever before, since you have much more autonomy over your activities than you did as a middle manager. The executive who was a financial man can develop tunnel vision by focusing on money matters; the executive who was an engineer may be so absorbed in the technical aspects of the company that he doesn't find time for personnel matters or the financing of new products. No one but yourself can blow the whistle on the way you compartmentalize your time.

Developing and maintaining this so necessary sense of balance will entail the quickest reaction time you have ever shown. Not only are the cues you receive subtle in the extreme; they are also, for the most part, of short duration. You will have to recognize them, weight and balance them, and determine the proper action or inaction in the blink of an eye. Remember, we are speaking now of the day-to-day routine of your position. Of course, you will have adequate time for the major policy decisions. But the executive's good judgment is often shown when he takes no action at all. This may be the deciding factor between running your job and being run by it. When your job runs you, you are on your way out.

Another important aspect of the executive's sense of balance is his attention to incoming communications. The best executives become famous as good listeners even more than as good talkers. The secret is that you learn so much more that way. You won't have the time or the energy to cover the whole physical area of your business often; the news has to be brought to you. Because of this, you are up against one of the major dangers to your security: How much of the information you receive has been screened to the advantage of those reporting to you? In other words, are you getting the straight story or only part of it? The security check on this problem once again lies in your sense of balance. You will have to weigh your incoming communications one against the other and check for discrepancies and apparent contradictions. If you find any, your investigation of them should be mercilessly thorough.

Your position in top management is most certainly one of kinetic equilibrium; there will never again be a static moment in your job if you are doing your work properly. In this connection, remember that it will be a long time after your arrival in the executive suite before you achieve the "Look, ma, no hands" situation. It will take both your hands, both your feet, and all of your mind to maintain that delicate balance over the complex structure under your control. The one last question then is: What do you do if you lose control for just a second and stumble badly? No one is perfect, and you certainly will make mistakes. When you do, your salvation rests entirely upon your ability to recover your balance quickly and smoothly—if possible, before your critics and rivals spot the error. A mistake rectified before it can be compounded is nearly the same as no mistake at all.

The real secret of maintaining your balance in your job is to keep your eyes squarely on the objective at all times, just as you keep your eyes on the road, not on the gas pedal, when you are driving your car.

How Many Mistakes Can You Afford Up There?

We said that an error quickly covered is almost the same as no error. Almost. The question remains: How many times might you be allowed to miss the mark when you are playing with everyone else's stakes? The answer is: Very few. Of course, in your situation, five to ten years might elapse before anyone could be certain that you made a boner, since executive decisions are not intended to hit their mark for about that span of time.

Priorities have been assigned to the kinds of mistakes an executive can make. The worst type is fiscal. When the money of the enterprise is directly involved, the attention of everyone is unwavering until the answer is forthcoming. This is purely self-preservation. When the money is gone, so is the company. Next is a tie between errors in launching new products and errors in the facilities planned and built to take care of those products. The third type of mistake concerns people. An executive is more likely to be forgiven an error in choosing personnel than in any other area. Perhaps this is tacit recognition that it is more difficult to make a valid judgment of people than of matters having to do with money or materials.

We have assumed that your experience as a supervisor and a middle manager has sharpened to a fine edge your general ability to make valid decisions. But you must protect yourself from inadvertent, and essentially silly, errors arising from your own ignorance. Perhaps we should now examine in brief some modern decision-making aids which can help you avoid making foolish errors.

In the first place, for all intents and purposes the day of the seat-of-the-pants decision is no more. Modern businesses now have access to tons of pertinent data. There is so much information, in fact, that the trouble lies in differentiating the important from the unimportant. It is here that you can make your first serious error—by trying to do all the winnowing yourself. This is an unjustifiable waste of your time and talents; it is to do this that you have gathered a staff of industrial engineers, systems people, and operations research experts. It is their job to feed to you pertinent information about current problems. Your part of the operation should be to designate alternatives and choose the best one to implement. However, if you are to be able to do this rationally, you must be well acquainted with the principles of the disciplines just mentioned. You must be satisfied in your mind that the data you receive are reasonable.

In this connection, it is time that the honeymoon between the American businessman and electronic data processing comes to an end. We have too many grim reminders of the havoc which results when unsophisticated executives blindly accept the computer. The other important factor about this esoteric discipline is the widespread lack of communication between the computer staff and clients. Some computer people seem deliberately to keep customers in the dark about what is really going on so as to simplify the process of building an empire and amassing power. It is time for management to demand meaningful communication with computer people. It would be better to go back to manual accounting than to be saddled with a monster that drinks incalculable amounts of your corporation's lifeblood.

Of one thing you may be certain: Every action you take as an executive will be scrutinized carefully by everyone who has the right to do so—and by many who do not. In the process, you will be subjected to many criticisms which are unjust but which hurt nevertheless. At your level, any accusation is of the utmost importance. By the time you answer it and show it to be false, the damage may be done. At the top, reputation is hardly ever distinguishable from character.

Although there is no denying the need to avoid mistakes, it must be said that if you worry about the possibility of making a mistake and therefore postpone or refuse to make necessary decisions, you are dead. You must plunge ahead and make a decision anyway, and live with the results. Your best defense will lie in learning everything you can about the techniques of decision making and in making the proper value judgments about when to employ each of them. It is here that you will have to show real expertise, and it is for this reason that you earn a large portion of your pay. Your promotion was an overt recognition of the confidence those in charge have placed in your abilities. Remember this. There will be moments when it will be highly supportive.

All reasonable people will know that you are the last one who wants to make a major error, since you would be the first to pay for it on the day of reckoning. In other words, your motivation is above suspicion. This should help immensely to keep a positive attitude in your thinking and general mental outlook. The importance of this is beyond calculation. The winner has to believe that he is going to win; the loser will question his ability to do so.

To summarize: Prepare yourself in the modern decision-making techniques. Use them. Make proper use of your staff rather than spinning your wheels or immersing yourself in senseless details. Put to use the expertise you have spent a lifetime acquiring. Keep your head. When the time comes, make your decision and be prepared to abide by it and its consequences. Your business career has demonstrated that you will win a lot more than you will lose; there is no reason to suspect that this established trend will be reversed when you become an executive. Your training and development activities have built-in safeguards against this contingency. Now, relax.

How Do You Know Whether You're Right?

If you have to accustom yourself to the necessity of always being right—of almost never being allowed an error —you become much concerned about how you arrive at a correct decision. The method accepted and used by most business leaders is to eliminate possible sources of error along the decision-making path. As you come to each point where alternative actions present themselves for choice, examine each of them closely and tag them in the order of their probability of failure. Scientists have used this method of forced comparisons and forced choices for many years with considerable success.

For example, let us say that you are about to decide whether to automate your manufacturing. The final go or no-go decision will be reached only after you have made a series of preliminary decisions. Is your present plant layout adaptable to automation without a complete rebuilding job? What is the payout for the cost of the new machinery? How much modification will have to be made in your warehouse and shipping departments? Do your financial people (or your bankers) believe the necessary money can be obtained for the project without too great a strain and too great a risk for the entire enterprise? How much retraining will be required for the people left after automation has been accomplished? Are your people prepared for the reduction in force to be effected at the changeover? Will you be faced with a long and costly strike as a result of the action? If so, are you prepared for a long war of attrition with your labor force? Have your sales people done the necessary market research? Will there be sales for the increased production you are planning?

Any one of these questions could possibly contain a fatal booby trap for the entire project unless you make the necessary decisions before proceeding. Too much is at stake to depend on your intuition for the answers to any of these questions.

One variable can cause you more trouble in decision making than any of the others: the element of time. For example, in the situation just mentioned, how long will the changeover take from manual to automated manufacturing? What will this lag do to your sales and your customer relations? Will you lose so many old customers because of a temporary lack of product that the net result will be disastrous? In your overall planning, have you built in an allowance for unforeseen, uncontrollable delays such as a strike in a key vendor's plant when you are waiting for new machinery from him?

You could say with reason that it begins to look as if you can't, and never will, know if you're right. If you are looking for brass-bound, copper-riveted certainties, this is true. As an executive, you are paid for being a risk-taker. So remind yourself once more that your procedure will be to reduce your chances of failure to the lowest possible point through careful decision making.

Incidentally, it is likely that you will be an executive for many years before you make a repetitive decision. Each situation you face for a long time will be new and unique, with very little historical data available to help you make your decision. Implicit in this is the need for extensive study of each problem as it arises. Start by making a list of the critical variables involved and giving them priorities. Then gather your data meticulously for each of them, and spend whatever time is necessary on each of the interim decisions leading to the final big one. Here too, time may be a critical factor. You may be forced, as you were while lower in the hierarchy, to come to a decision before you feel ready to do so. This adds much excitement—or anxiety, depending upon your makeup—to your working climate.

Although you alone will bear the ultimate responsibility for the choice you make, you would be foolhardy to be completely arbitrary and unilateral in your decisions. You do have many resource people to turn to along the way. They can often point out errors you overlooked in your absorption with the total picture. Moreover, we should once more reinforce the fact that you are now more involved than ever in a team effort. There is no point in carefully handpicking a group of associates unless you make full use of their assorted knowledge and expertise. Your judgment will be much better if you maintain an overview of what they are doing at your direction to help you come to the proper choice of action.

For your personal well-being, keep the work going at a smooth, even pace all the time. You will feel more comfortable and will have a much better chance of being right if you keep plugging along, rather than alternating between quiescent periods and bursts of furious activity. Like the professional athlete, you must never let yourself get out of condition. A sustained, steady flow of activity will reduce your anxiety level to manageable proportions. This is true of your staff as well. If they see you quietly going about your business day by day, they will follow your example, and you will have a team in actuality as well as in name.

You will never know you're right until long after the fact of making your decision, but, as we have indicated, there is a well-defined method for reducing the risk of error to a reasonable level. By so doing, you can create an atmosphere in which to work with the prospect of achieving some solid results. This is naturally one of your major objectives on the job and always will be. Once you form the habit for this type of operation, you will become a functioning executive, with a much better than even chance of continuing success.

Now, Who's Your Coach?

As an executive, if you do your job well, you will be running your own game more than you ever have before. There will be fewer people in a position to question your actions, and probably not more than one or two people in the entire organization will give you direct orders. This new freedom will be heady at first, and you could be forgiven a few weeks of running a little wild. But of course you won't, because of the effect it would have on those who work for you, and you have never had greater need for a smoothly running work group. You need them at least as much as they need your leadership.

But even the top man needs someone to turn to for

general counseling. For example, you will want a sounding board for those new projects and great ideas before they are actually implemented. Are they really that good, or have you overlooked a fatal flaw somewhere in the concept?

It could be downright embarrassing to begin a big campaign, and then have a junior member of middle management point out why it will never fly. The right kind of coach can help you firm up the entire idea and flesh it out so that it will be sure to go.

Unless you are the chief executive officer, there will be a person to whom you nominally report, according to the organization chart. Ordinarily, this man would automatically become your mentor. However, it is not too unusual these days to have total delegation at the executive level. Your nominal boss may tell you to go ahead and make your own decisions, since that is what you were hired to do. If he takes this stance, he has automatically removed himself from the category of coach, and you will have to turn elsewhere.

You could do much worse than to use a "committee," a team of other executives or trusted members of middle management, many of whom you have known and respected for years. Some companies have gone formally into a structure of team management at the top level, on the theory that no one man can be expected to have the expertise necessary in all functions and fields to run the whole enterprise. If you don't want to go that far, have the informal committee for counsel on important problems. If you work at it for a little time, this procedure can become quite functional. In your meetings with the committee, you must establish once and for all an open, relaxed atmosphere. Every member of the team must feel free to say whatever he thinks, knowing there will be no reprisal from anyone whose feelings he may happen to bruise. The procedure should be a controlled brainstorming session—plus. At first, collect all ideas without judgment; then, before the meeting is over, start the process of judging, picking and choosing those elements that seem most promising. It is understood, however, that carrying out or implementing anything decided in this meeting will be the work of your regular staff people, not the committee. This group's next concern would be to evaluate the outcome of a project. A group post-mortem can be a fine learning experience.

It is unlikely that this device, functional and helpful though it may be, will really take the place of an individual coach. You will probably want to search one out and enlist his aid and comfort from here on. It is not mandatory that he be in the same business. In fact, there might be advantages to you if he is not. His would be a fresh, unbiased approach to your problems, uncluttered with hang-ups common to those who work in your field. But it is essential that he be a man whose perception and judgment you can wholeheartedly respect. He must also have the strength of character to say *no* to you frequently and even peremptorily. Not that he will make your decisions, but he must be given the privilege of sounding off when he thinks you are wrong. Without this ground rule, there would be no purpose to the whole exercise.

If this relationship is purely professional, the matter of his remuneration should be settled early and definitively. He will probably want either an annual retainer or an hourly fee, and don't be surprised if he quotes a price of $100 to $150 per hour for his time. Whether you consider this an expense of your business and charge it back to the company, or whether you think it is your personal responsibility, is a question for you to work out with your company management. In either event, if you find the right man, the cost will be insignificant in light of the results achieved.

One inescapable aspect of this relationship is that your mentor will come to know as much about your business as any actual employee. The ethical aspects here are delicate, but clear. Your guide, whoever he may be, must be worthy of your complete trust and his professionalism must be impeccable. Otherwise, you could be letting yourself in for insupportable difficulties over a period of time. Lack of a clearly defined and universally accepted code of ethics to which all members subscribe is one reason why management is still not classified as a true profession. This code will have to be established, and soon. It should be occupying the minds of all real managers to a considerable degree. True professionalism cannot be legislated, because it is a positive rather than a negative force. It is composed of things you do, rather than things you are prohibited from doing. More widespread understanding of this fact will lead to acceptance of the responsibility of the true manager.

Is the Prize Worth the Game?

Your development plan has now been carried right up to the moment of your promotion. If you are going to change your mind about taking on additional responsibilities and making yourself much more vulnerable, do so before you accept an executive position. There would be much comment from your associates if you were to refuse the job at the last moment. Some of this comment you would hear, and considerably more of it would be made in your absence. But this little storm would be nothing compared to the gale which would blow up if you were to resign shortly after accepting top responsibility. Although, as we have said, you can never really know what the job is like until you are in it, you would be far better off not to take it if you still have the slightest doubt about it. Only if the excitement of the prospect is overpowering should you go ahead, because only then can you be fairly sure that you will find challenge rather than threat in the problems of the executive job.

One thing is certain. There is no other place in the business or industrial world so filled with successive chances for satisfying your self-actualization needs. In the process of doing an acceptable job as an executive, you will grow and develop more than you ever have before. If you should become an outstanding executive, you will not recognize yourself after a few years in this environment. If there is within you the slightest need to feel that you have made a contribution to your fellow man by having been here, there is no better place to do it in than the tough arena that is the habitat of the executive.

Whether you are manufacturing a product or purveying a service, so long as what you do is honest and honorable you can hold your head high in any group and defy anyone to denigrate your position or your actions. Moreover, as an executive you will be a leader and will contribute to the general design of your surroundings. More than that, you will be one of the stabilizers in a society which gives indication now and then of considerable indecision as to its ultimate objectives. By your leadership and example, you can help many people to gain or regain a proper perspective on their lives.

Of course there will be pressures, and of course you will have your bad moments, or bad days, or bad weeks. You wouldn't want it to be too easy, would you? These will be the stimulants to your best performance, the touch of the whip that elicits the last, winning burst of energy from any thoroughbred. Beating your competition to the tape is the biggest and best reward you will get out of that new job you have worked so hard for.

Now is the time for your greatest concentration on the major goals of your enterprise. You can't afford to let yourself be distracted by anything. Your singleness of purpose must be unwavering. Mental discipline, emotional maturity, hard work, and just the slightest dash of good luck will give you an unbeatable edge.

*　　*　　*

The central theme of this chapter has been your chances of success after you have been promoted to the executive echelon. One of the most necessary ingredients is that you like the climate there. You can't really know this until you try it, but some clues which can be highly indicative should be examined now.

Because of the many vectors which will be operating upon you, your sense of balance will be more important than ever. Your position will be one of kinetic equilibrium; if you ever become static in an executive position, you are done for.

You will be allowed few mistakes as an executive. You will be the guardian of a large percentage of the net worth of the enterprise, and your decisions must be right nearly every time. In this connection, some criteria were examined which will tell you your chances for being right in the decisions you make before you implement them. You should use these tests assiduously before committing yourself to any major project.

When you become an executive, you will probably need to choose a new coach to whom you can turn for help in solving your problems. This choice is critical to your success as a top manager. Someone outside the organization is often most functional in this role.

Finally, before you take the job, you must once and for all allay any doubts about doing it. Remember, the rewards of the executive's life are big, and they are real. If you choose to go ahead, you will enter the best part of your life.

11

What Does an Executive Owe to Society?

HOW far does your citizenship go? This question would stimulate more argument among management people today than it did a generation ago. At that time, the more cynical businessman would have denied categorically that his citizenship had anything to do with the business world. Like his religion, his personal association with his city, state, and country were kept in a compartment entirely separate from his work. He saw nothing at all contradictory in a dual or even triple set of ethical values. He could therefore approach his fellow man in one way at church, in another way in his civic relationships, and in still another way at work. Many a manager simplified the situation to the utmost by not recognizing employees as people. His attitude toward them was somewhat like that of the lord of the manor toward his serfs. Thus no moral opprobrium was ever attached to the most blatant exploitation of those who worked for him.

It is unfortunate that this attitude still exists in some backward enterprises. But they will almost certainly disappear in the near future, simply because they will no longer be able to get people to work for them. Because of the impact of McGregor's Theory Y and the findings of modern behavioral scientists, the manager has been forced to recognize that his machines are operated by living, breathing, sensitive human beings and that he must take them into consideration in designing and implementing policy. Unless he does, his business cannot remain competitive, and he will fail.

This change in management's attitude represents progress, but it is not the whole story. What remains to be kindled and made active is a recognition that the responsibilities of running a business are directed not only inward to the stockholders and employees, but also outward to the rest of society. A business which does not contribute something positive to society has no right to continue. This little morsel has been known to cause some businessmen to gag and choke a little. Some economists have written and spoken endlessly in an attempt to rationalize the existence of some businesses which take away from society rather than contribute to it. Their most frequent (and most specious) argument is that "the people will find this situation somewhere, so let's keep it out in the open where we have more control over it."

You, as an executive, will have the same duties of citizenship in your office or factory as you do in the voting booth or in your church. If and when your manufacturing process emits harmful substances into the environment, you have a simple choice: Correct the nuisance or abandon the manufacturing process. Man's ingenuity is great enough to rise to any ecological challenge he faces in providing a product to a technological society. There is no such thing as an insuperable difficulty in maintaining a safe living climate.

As an executive, your citizenship extends far enough to force you to face situations within your enterprise which are actually or potentially harmful. If you make a deal with a union to do something which subverts the public weal, you are a bad citizen. Short weights, mislabeling, deceptive packaging, substitution of ingredients less than specification, delivery of products which do not meet quality standards—the list can be extended indefinitely of business practices which are evidences of bad citizenship. As an executive, you will have both the responsibility and the authority to correct these evils as you discover them. You can even do so for a selfish reason: If you don't, outside authorities will eventually force you to do so.

Business immorality has a harmful effect on the company. No man has ever been clever enough to hide from his employees the fact that he is cutting corners in a way that will hurt someone else. You may argue that a significant number of your employees may have less than admirable characters, and that you would actually be conforming to their norms if you were to do some of these things. Perhaps. But why should you conform to a standard you know to be wrong, simply because some of those

217

around you are doing so? You are now a leader, and your actions will be scrutinized minutely by many people, whether you like it or not. In fact, they will point to you as justification for their own behavior.

Once the standard has been established and your general policy in these matters formulated, your actual performance as an executive will become easier. For the most part, you can base your major business decisions on ethical and moral considerations; once you have done so, your decision has been made for you. The trick lies in making sure you are using logic, not sophistry, in spelling out the elements of your problem. You are smart enough intellectually to be able to rationalize in almost any surroundings; your citizenship duties as a modern executive forbid you to do so. From time to time you can expect to meet severe opposition within your organization from extremists and opportunists. They will gang up on you, and the confrontation may be formidable. So what? Ever since you joined management, you have enjoyed a good fight—when you knew you were right.

You may also have to undertake and follow through on a serious reeducation of some of your superiors, those who still believe in the dog-eat-dog manner of doing business. It's up to you to convince them that their way will no longer work.

When Is Profit No Longer Profit?

It is easy to offer a flip, smart retort to the question of when profit is no longer profit, but there is no place for cynicism in an executive's thinking about the profits of his enterprise. His responsibility is unequivocal and unceasing. If you are an executive in a profit-making organization, it is your duty to maximize those profits whenever you can do so honestly and with integrity. Similarly, if you work for a nonprofit organization, your duty is to get maximum efficiency and render maximum service within your budget.

But profit is not profit when you fail to rise to your full stature as a citizen in conducting your business. If your firm does not make a positive contribution to society, or if it in any way harms any group of people, you are not making a profit—you are practicing extortion. You make a profit if you increase the net worth of your organization without harming anyone associated with you, particularly the customer. It is entirely possible to make a net profit of 25, 50, or 100 percent and do it honestly, if your product is satisfying the customer's real need at a price he can afford. Therein lies the standard for the accrual of profit: the ability of the customer to pay without doing himself harm. In other situations it is entirely possible that a profit of 1 percent would be excessive and that the group involved should be restrained from further trade. The ability to pay implies more than the presence of ready cash. Also to be considered are the long-range effects on the welfare of the customer and the possible depletion of his assets at an unfavorable rate.

This latter consideration is applicable to your own situation as well as to the customer's. If quick cash is accumulated in your treasury by a reckless compromising of your own future assets, this obviously is also not a profitable exercise. In fact, many projects are launched with the full understanding that the best to be hoped for, for several years, would be a breakeven operation. You, as the executive, are in the best position to make this kind of decision. The difference between yesterday's Scrooge and today's enlightened manager is the latter's understanding of his duty to himself, his enterprise, and society at large, in about equal proportions. We do not live in isolation.

Without question, your duty is clear: to examine the profitability of any contemplated change in your operation. The continued existence and health of your enterprise depends upon the flow of new money into your coffers as a net result of all your activity. But you are the quality control member of your team, and you are aware of a dichotomy in your perspective and the necessity for a broader viewpoint of the comparative good for you, for the customer, and for the community. Your total environment has clearly defined rights, although many of them may never have any direct connection with your operation, either as customer or vendor.

This is not a decision which can be made once, or with extreme attention and effort on your part, and then be conveniently forgotten. There is change in the components of the mix, and every time they change, you must reevaluate the entire process. In a real sense, this continuing monitoring is purely defensive. Each generation is more sophisticated in this area than the previous one, and its judgment of your actions will be sharp and incisive. You will have to defend whatever position you assume with every argument at your command—and with all the supporting data you can muster. Your word is your check, but it must be backed by money in the bank.

It is essential for you to remember that there is more

to profit than money. A generation ago, some forward-looking sociologists and economists added a new term to our lexicon: "psychic income." You can contribute profit to others, and realize it yourself, in many ways other than fiscal. It seems incredible to the layman that a singer, a dancer, or an actor can command astronomical sums from the public, but the public has always been glad to bestow riches upon the outstanding minstrel and mime. Whether a man ever verbalizes it or not, he is fundamentally glad to pay through the nose for momentary relief from the drabness of his daily life and for a short trip into the excitement of a make-believe but happier world.

There are many facets to the gem of profit, but the luster of the whole can be dimmed by one tiny flaw, and the value of the stone lost. You may not have been aware of it, but for several years past you have been undergoing a metamorphosis into a generalist. Your duty and your area of responsibility now blanket the entire business; there is no part of it which you can safely ignore in order to concentrate on a favorite segment. A vector in one direction must always be counterbalanced, for the sake of the kinetic equilibrium of the whole.

This larger picture of citizenship is worthy of top priority among your executive duties. It will not be easy to weight the components or to fit them together so that you can live and operate easily with the idea. Nevertheless, nothing is more important to your initial or ongoing success than this expanded consciousness. It must become a conditioned reflex throughout your operation as an executive. Profit is really profitable only when it redounds to the good of all parties signatory to the agreement. If one member is shortchanged, the entire process is bankrupt.

Whom Does the Executive Lead?

The question of whom you lead as an executive could easily be given the simplistic answer that the executive leads his people. But the truth is not nearly as easy as this. People must acknowledge and accept their nominal leaders before leadership can be effective. Thus, in a large corporation, no executive can be the leader of all his people. He will be lucky if a majority of the employees follows him in all his decisions and ventures. The smart executive knows that he exerts true leadership over those who report directly to him; he hopes that management will be able to pass this leadership down the line, level by level. It is extremely difficult for an hourly employee, seven levels below in the hierarchy, to feel personal leadership exerted on him by an executive he may never have met. This is not to say that it cannot be done, but it is a difficult task that requires a charismatic leader.

From the standpoint of society, you will exhibit your most important leadership as an executive outside your business activities. The influence generated by your position will spread over a surprisingly large area. Many people whose names you do not know will be influenced by your actions and your public pronouncements. This will at first be hard for you to believe. It takes some doing for a manager to get used to being a public figure. Because of this power, you must exercise extreme care in the things you say and do. Your social influence within your environment begins at this point and will continue to grow as long as you remain in your job. If you become an executive by the time you are 50, you will probably exert an influence on two generations of the public before you retire.

And, like Bernard Baruch, your influence may be greater after you retire.

The most critical facet of this leadership activity will be your public speaking. You will receive many invitations to speak to groups. Eventually, you will have to limit these occasions because they drain your strength and energies. Yet it is good public relations to respond to many of the requests you receive. The danger lies in the fact that you no longer have a one-to-one relationship with your audience. Because you cannot see their faces, you cannot judge from their expressions and other nonverbal cues the effect of your words. You can only guess—often with poor results —what the overall effect of your message is. Your feedback will be delayed and probably garbled, so that you may never know exactly what your reception was, unless some dramatic (and usually unfavorable) reaction is evoked. Then, of course, comes the well-known repairing of the broken dikes.

You would be well advised to make use of your enterprise's public relations people every time you appear before the public. There are two ways to do this: You can let a public relations man write your speeches for you, or you can write them yourself and subject them to the censorship and advice of the public relations people. Your choice is solely a matter of personal preference; properly handled, either way will be functional. Whichever method you choose, listen to your advisers. This is their area of expertise; they are paid to be knowledgeable. One word of caution: whatever the pressures of the day, never go to the dais with a speech that you haven't read at least several times. Nothing can make you look more inept than a bad reading of another man's words; it will do grave damage to your public image and that of your employer. Incidentally, total veto power over the subject matter of a given speech will still be your responsibility. No one else is in as good a position as you are to choose your topic.

Because of the various constraints upon you at this time, you should start to be highly selective about the outside activities in which you participate. It is here that you retain personal control over the amount of influence you will have on your society through your leadership. You may even have to make the unpleasant decision to pull out of an activity of public service you have enjoyed for many years to take on another one which your analysis tells you is of greater importance. For example, if you have been an enthusiastic worker in scouting, you may have to quit that job to take on the general chairmanship of the community fund drive for the next year. And you may have to drop that after a year's hard work to become a member of the urban planning board for your community. You must keep the matter of relative importance in proper perspective so that you can do your best in discharging your social responsibilities as an executive.

You must also be selective about the number of outside activities you take on. There is an ever present danger that your goodwill could get you into trouble on the job. Only you can blow the whistle on your acceptance or rejection of outside service assignments. It would be easy to let them become an albatross around your neck, with your job performance becoming the principal casualty. Naturally, you cannot afford to let this happen.

One thing is evident. You should not accept a single added duty unless you are prepared to do a bang-up job on it. You have never been content with second-rate performance, and you shouldn't change that attitude now. Your stature and reputation as an executive will demand this selective judgment on your part, as well as the strength to act according to your considered answer.

Does the Executive Dare Control?

This question is not as foolish as it sounds. A generation ago, the owner of a business would have been mightily angered at the mere suggestion that he had anything less than total control. In the past few years, a significant change has become apparent in the attitudes of employees. Subservience toward any dictum of the boss has been replaced by a readiness to question vigorously any action of management which employees think is an infringement on their personal rights. In companies whose employees are union members, the union's strength enables employees to confront their boss directly in any conflict.

We are not suggesting that this climate should make you retreat from a confrontation, or that you should entertain any notion of abdicating your authority. You are being paid to run the business. But on many occasions a full conflict with the entire labor force might occur over a matter whose importance does not warrant it. To keep the ship going toward port, you will find it necessary to be selective about the issues on which you will stand fast with the full weight of the enterprise behind you.

There is another cogent reason why you, personally, should not get directly into some disagreements. That is the delegation of authority to levels of management which report to you. You will certainly want to avoid any action which gives the appearance (rightly or wrongly) of undercutting your subordinates by bypassing them. They have their show to run; let them do it, at least until they get in over their heads and indicate a need for your help. Remember, your present station means that you are no longer in the thick of the action; you make the policy, and middle management will implement it. The signal for you to get actively involved in items of control is your subordinates' failure, after a reasonable time, to make reasonable progress. Then, of course, you must take direct action of the most fundamental nature.

There will be much temptation for you to impose your self-image as the boss on many of your community and public service activities, even if you are serving in an advisory capacity. Whatever controls you do institute must be innocuous, and the hand holding the reins must be invisible. You must restrain your normal impatience to see immediate and quantifiable results in these areas. Your effectiveness in service outside your enterprise will be a measure of your influence rather than of your direct power. You will be called upon to persuade rather than to direct.

In a sense, you will have to practice persuasion in your regular business life too. You will be required to get agreement from your own people in many situations by persuasive measures rather than by simple edict or fiat. The more mature and sophisticated our society becomes, the more this will be true in general business and industrial practice. The whip hand has been the object of open and direct attack many times within the past few years, and that trend is increasing.

The most powerful control you can ever exert will be through your ability to make your people understand and accept your objectives as their own. When this happens, you have their direct and personal involvement, as well as at least a modicum of commitment to achieving those goals. And this, after all, is the main purpose of all your personal business activities.

As the nerve center for the outward communications of your company, you must be in fine tune with both your people and those outside the gates. As a change agent you have the moral responsibility to transmit to the rest of the citizenry those products or services developed in your organization which you find good for you and which you think would also be functional for society at large. You will not have the personal power to impose these things upon the public, but it is part of your job to make the effort to win acceptance for them.

Thus you most certainly do dare to control, but you must do so in a much more sophisticated manner than your predecessor used.

How Does the Executive Shape Society?

As an executive, you will help to shape the society in which you live by several means. The changes and innovations which you initiate and pass on to your people will have an effect on them and their surroundings. Each adaptation we make to newness in our environment alters our group relationships. Therefore, it is up to you to consider carefully all possible results of any new ideas you propose to initiate in your organization. Not only will your group be transformed, but it will pass some of that transformation to its surroundings.

227

You also act as a catalyst and nerve center for passing along changes coming from other organizations. You may want to modify new procedures as they impinge on your people. There could be many reasons for doing this, but the basic one is that different groups will react in different ways to the same stimulus.

Because of your position of power, you have a duty to do some deep and extensive planning for the changes you institute. Your objectives should be clearly delineated in your own thinking, whether or not you see fit to communicate them. Unless you can see that a specific improvement for your people is inherent in a proposal, you should not accept it. Change can be traumatic for those involved; it must not be instituted whimsically. You should be economical of your group's reservoir of energy. This planning duty has another serious implication for you: that you must become familiar with the elements of sociology, as well as economics. Our society has become unbelievably complex. It is your role to reduce this complexity by making necessary changes within your group as smooth and pleasant as possible. This will not be a solo effort; your associates must be deeply involved in the entire process but getting that involvement will require your ingenuity in action.

Can You Stand Up to the Challenge?

The functioning executive in today's business world has a task greater than any businessman has ever faced before. The scope of your responsibility is wider and deeper, and it will be more so as time goes on. Remember, however, that the job of the executive will continue to be done by men and women, and what others can do, you can do. You have every opportunity on the job to create a lasting personal memorial for yourself.

Your esteem in the community will come from the contributions you make to better living. We see everywhere comforting signs of a full-blown sense of social responsibility among executives. They are building this into the warp and woof of their daily business life. And, in so doing, they are involving themselves and their people in an evolutionary process which will result in a better world.

Index

aggression, response to, 106–109
ambition, in supervisor or manager, 4
animosity
    against new executive, 93–113
    reaction to, 96–100, 106–109
anxiety
    control of, 148–149
    hobby as reducer of, 13
    timetable activity of, 187
anxiety level, 135–154
    dislike of others in, 147–150
    inventory of, 147–150
    management stakes and, 64–65
Argyris, Chris, 101
assets, risking of, 156–158
associates
    replacement of, 126
    tests for, 122–123
automation, decision making and, 205

balance
    communication and, 200–201
    sure instinct for, 198–201
Baruch, Bernard, 223
base camp
    "security" of, 56–74
    temptation to remain at, 15–34
betting
    odds calculation in, 164–168
    risks and rewards in, 155–164
boss
    as confidant, 181–182
    face saving for, 59–62
    game plan and, 191–192
    middle manager differentiated from, 79–80
    paternalism of, 192
    see also superior; top management
brainstorming sessions, 47
    decision making and, 210
    rules of, 165
business immorality, 217

challenge, to new executive, 228–229
changes
    executive's milestones of, 78
    forecasting of, 124–127
    profitability and, 220
    rationale for, 48
    see also innovation
checkups, medical, 85, 151–152
citizenship
    duties of, 217
    limits of, 215
    profit and, 219
colleagues, as confidants, 182
committee, counseling by, 208–209
communication(s)
    balance and, 200–201
    executive as center of, 227
    executive isolation and, 29
    between middle manager and subordinates, 130–133

trust and confidence in, 132
communications ring, harmful rumors and, 94
company assets, risking of, 158–161
competition
    in executive, 109
    long-range planning and, 118–119
    "reading of" by executive, 117–121
    risk management and, 168
conceptual skill, need for, 127–130
confidant(s)
    boss as, 181–182
    committee as, 208–209
    risks taken with, 184
confidence, *see* trust
control, forms of, 225–227
coordination, in managerial coup, 57
costs, in managerial coup, 57
criticism, sensitivity to, 88

decision making
    error elimination in, 205–208
    techniques of, 204
    variables in, 206
development program
    personnel selection and, 124–127
    self-inventory of, 3
    supervisor and, 2
    see also planning; self-evaluation
doctor, medical reports from, 85, 151–153

economic decisions, team effort in, 51
economics
    expertise in, 81
    middle manager's knowledge of, 49–52
electronic data processing, 203
enemies
    handling of, 93–95
    personalizing attacks of, 103–105
entrepreneur, new role of, 43
executive
    acceptance of position by, 211–212

executive (*continued*)
    ambition in, 4
    anxiety level of, 135–154
    in "arena of champions," 99
    atmosphere and milieu of, 35–55
    autonomy of, 109
    challenge to, 229
    changes forecast by, 124–127
    citizenship duties of, 217
    communication by, 130–133
    as "communications center," 227
    community esteem and, 222–223, 229
    company assets and, 158–161
    competitive nature of, 109
    conceptual skill in, 127–130
    confidence risks in, 183
    control by, 225–227
    counseling for, 208–211
    cover-up for, 59–62
    "crystal ball" of, 114–134
    dangerous ploys of, 178
    debt of to society, 215–229
    decision making by, 204–208
    defensive action in risk management, 166–167
    desire to be liked, 147–150
    development program of, 124–127
    deviations from norm by, 38
    economic decisions and, 51
    and electronic data processing, 203
    enemies of, 102
    esteem and reputation as motivation in, 168
    family relationships of, 144–147
    fatalistic attitude in, 180, 187
    forecasting by, 114–134
    former subordinates as peers of, 65–68
    frustration of, 121–122
    game plan of, 174–194
    good health in, 85, 151–153
    introspection in, 54
    intuition in, 115
    irritation flash point of, 138–141
    isolation of, 28–31, 36, 77, 179–180, 196

executive (*continued*)
    as leader, 222–225
    "letting go" in, 104
    life-style changes in, 76–78
    long chance taken by, 161–164
    loss of friendship by, 31–33
    mental toughness of, 86–89
    middle manager's contacts with, 37–38
    "milestone of changes" for, 78
    mistakes of, 201–205
    and motivations of others, 100–103
    new trends and, 116–117
    odds calculation in risk management by, 164–168
    operations research and, 43
    organizational analysis by, 83
    organization formed by, 78–79
    personal chances taken by, 156–158
    personal files and records for, 82
    personality changes in, 76
    personalization of business activities by, 53
    personnel selection by, 121–124
    persuasion by, 226
    physical toughness of, 84–86
    planning and, 62–65, 228
    positive attitude of, 141
    power of, 25, 228
    profit and, 219–221
    public relations and, 223
    public service and, 224
    reading of competition by, 117–119
    repetitive decisions by, 206–207
    resignation of, 197
    responsibility in, 199, 207, 228–229
    self-actualization for, 99, 212
    self-confidence of, 45, 110–112
    self-control in, 103
    self-evaluation by, *see* self-evaluation
    self-image of, 226
    sense of balance in, 198–201
    sleep habits of, 136–138
    shaping of society by, 227–229
    "sniping" at, 93–113

executive (*continued*)
   subordinate selection by, 44
   as symbol, 103
   as tactician or strategist, 42–43
   temper in, 138–140
   time-outs allowed to, 188–190
   total isolation of, 28–31, 36, 77, 179–180, 196
   vacation for, 53, 141–144
   value of risk to, 168–170
   as winner or loser, 171–173
   see also middle manager; supervisor
executive committee, 209
executive level
   ambition and, 4
   middle manager's contacts with, 37–38
   power at, 25, 228
   vacancies at, 12
executive ranks
   life style in, 76–78, 195–196
   remaining in, 195–214
   unpleasant side of, 196–197
exercise, need for, 85

face saving, for boss, 59–62
family relationships
   planning timetable and, 186–187
   preparation of family for impending change, 13
   quality of, 144–147
   see also wife
files and records, need for, 82
forecasting, art of, 114–134
friends, retention of, 31–33

gambling, compulsive, 168–169
   see also risk management
game plan, 174–194
   see also planning
goals
   achievement of, 176
   knowledge of, 175–177
   motivation and, 100–103
group, rapport with, 5

group consultation, 209–210
growth, personal, *see* personal growth
gymnasium exercise, 85

health care, need for, 85, 151–153
health club, exercise at, 85
Herzberg, Frederick, 16 n., 100–101
hobbies
    in anxiety reduction, 13
    for top management, 53
home, care in choice of, 13
home life, job situation and, 146–147
    see also family relationships; wife
honesty
    degrees of, 69
    need for, 68–71
hostility
    competitiveness and, 109
    response to, 106–109
human nature, constancy of, 99
humility, need for, 59

individuals, rapport with, 5
industry survey, innovations and, 47
information, security and, 39–40
innovation
    middle management and, 6–7, 45–48
    planning and, 47
    resistance to, 48
introspection, need for, 54
intuition, process of, 115
irritation flash point, 138–141
isolation
    of executive, 28–31, 36, 77, 179–180
    reaction to, 196

job analysis, by supervisor or manager, 9–11
job description, personnel and, 9
job knowledge, importance of, 8–11
job pressure, reaction to, 196
    see also anxiety

leader
  advice sought from, 7
  confrontation and, 6
  executive as, 222–225
  vs. group, 5
  temper control in, 140
leadership
  inner direction in, 76
  qualities of, 4–7
  society and, 222–223
"letting go," danger of, 104
losing, anatomy of, 171

Machiavellian politics, 23
management, entrance into, 1
management consultant, use of, 210–211
management development, 2
  see also development program; planning
management trainee, 2
manager
  as leader, 4–7
  middle, *see* middle manager
  seminars for, 11–12
  strengths and weaknesses of, 3
  trust of personnel by, 10
managerial coup
  anxiety level and, 64–65
  elements of, 56–57
managerial talent, nurturing of by supervisor, 66
Maslow, Abraham, 99–100
materials and machinery, "risking" of, 158–161
matrix organization, 9
McGregor, Douglas, 10, 100, 216
medical checkups, need for, 85, 151–152
medical report, from doctor, 151–152
mental discipline, need for, 213
mental toughness, 86–89
middle management, advancement in, 3
middle manager
  advantages of remaining as, 15–34
  anxiety level of, 135–154

assistance seeking in, 182–183
big-time politics for, 22–25
communications with subordinates, 21
confidants of, 181–184
contacts with top management, 35–38
contrasted with subordinates, 77–79
covering up mistakes by, 201
cultivation of people by, 66–67
dangerous ploys of, 178–179
"differences" in, 75–91
differentiated from boss, 79–80
discretionary time of, 188–189
economics knowledge of, 49–52
fatalistic attitude in, 187
fear of vacation in, 141–142
former subordinates as peers of, 65–68
friends retained by, 31–33
future for, 19–20
game plan of, 174–194
goal of, 175–177
health needs of, 85, 151–153
humility in, 59
innovation in, 6–7, 45–48
leadership in, 18
long-odds chances by, 161–162
medical checkups for, 85, 151–152
mental toughness of, 86–89
mistakes by, 89–91
and motivations of others, 100–103
as "old pro," 71–74
peer competition for, 80–84
personal dislike of, 147–150
personality change in, 26
physical toughness in, 84–86
policy-making image in, 16
positive outlook of, 91
power needs of, 25–31
promotability of, 19–20
risk management and, 155
self-study and self-portrait of, 79–84, 89–90, 99,
    128–129, 212

middle manager (*continued*)
  stake in company, 52–55
  team procedures and, 18
  time-outs left for, 188–190
  timetable for, 184–187
  top-secret meetings and, 39–42
  total isolation and, 28–31
  wife and family relationships of, 145–147
  see also executive; supervisor
mistakes
  covering up of, 201
  by middle management, 89–90
  number allowed executive, 201–205
motivation
  esteem and reputation as, 168
  theory of, 100–103

operations research, 43
opportunism, danger of, 218
organization
  infiltration of by enemies, 94–95
  matrix type of, 9
  personality cult and, 79
  PERT/time chart of, 98
organizational analysis, by new executive, 83
organization chance, secret meetings and, 40–41
organizing function, job descriptions and, 9

paternalism, in superior, 192
patience, need for, 181
peer competition, self-evaluation and, 80–84
perfectionist, "miscasting" of, 191
performance, self-evaluation in, 73
  see also self-evaluation
personal assets, risking of, 156–158
personal attacks, evaluation of, 103–106
personal "betting," 155–158
personal convictions, value of, 105–106
personal dislikes, in others, 147–150
personal growth
  future success and, 21
  self-actualization and, 99, 212

personalities, in attacks on executive, 103–105
personality change
   at accession to big time, 26
   nature of, 76
personality cult, in organization formation, 79
personal motivation, theory of, 100–103
personnel problems, job descriptions and, 9
personnel selection, art of, 121–124
PERT/time, 63, 98
physical examinations, 84, 151–153
planning
   boss's role in, 191–192
   competition and, 118–119
   confidants in, 181–184
   daily review of, 127
   goals and, 175–177
   innovations and, 47
   job knowledge and, 8
   in managerial coup, 57–58
   by new executive, 62–65
   new trends and, 117
   power and, 228
   prize vs. effort in, 211–212
   timetable in, 184–187
   at top-secret meetings, 39
   of vacations, 143–144
polarization, supervision and, 8
policy making, urge toward, 16
political debts, 23
politics
   loner in, 24
   middle manager's aspirations and, 22–24
power
   at executive level, 25
   lust for, 16–17
   planning and, 228
prediction, by executive, 124–127
present job, attractions of, 15–21
problems, responsibility in face of, 199
professionalism, cultivation of people as, 66–67

profit
   citizenship and, 219
   failure of or limitations in, 218–221
   reevaluation of, 220–221
progress, management attitude toward, 216
promotability, of middle manager, 20–21
promotion
   anxiety about, 11–12, 150
   prize vs. effort in, 211–212
   responsibilities and, 53
   timetable in, 185–187
psychic income, 221
public relations department, 223
public service, importance of, 224

reaction time, in "sniping" situations, 96–100
records and files, need for, 82
responsibility
   decision making and, 207
   at executive level, 199, 228–229
risk management, 155
   defensive tactics in, 166–167
   odds in, 164–168
   timing in, 162–163
   value judgments in, 165
risk taking, winning or losing in, 171–173
rumor mongering, proper reaction to, 93–96

secret meetings, exclusion from, 39–40
   security, information control and, 39–40
   self-actualization, need for, 99, 212
   self-confidence, 45, 110–112
   self-control
      in personal attacks, 103
      self-confidence and, 111–112
   self-determination, performance standards and, 73
   self-direction, need for, 73
   self-evaluation
      conceptual skill and, 128–129
      major accomplishments in, 56
      by middle manager, 56
      mistakes noted in, 89–90

by new executive, 75–91
peer competition in, 80–84
performance standards and, 73–74
seminars, preparation through, 11
sleep habits, anxiety level and, 136–138
society
planning and, 228
shaping of by executive, 222, 227–229
strategy, vs. tactics, 42–45
subordinate
face saving by, 59–62
manager's differences from, 77–79
middle manager and, 17
as peers of executive, 66–68
superior, listening to, 11
see also boss; top management
superiority complex, 171
supervisor
dead end for, 19–20
job knowledge in, 8–11
leadership in, 5–6
managerial talent nurtured by, 66
personnel problems of, 2
temptation to remain at base camp, 15–34
urge to become executive, 1
see also middle manager; executive

tactics, vs. strategy, 42–45
team management, 209
technical and scientific personnel, polarization and, 8
temper, control of, 138–139
tests, for associates or subordinates, 122–123
Theory X and Theory Y, 10, 216
time-outs, number allowed in management advance,
188–189
timetable, need for, 184–187
timing, in managerial coup, 57
top management
artificial atmosphere and, 38
hobbies and, 53
middle manager's knowledge of, 35–36
team or committee work and, 209

top-secret meetings, new executive and, 39–42
trends, spotting of, 115–117
trust
   by and for manager, 68–71
   communication and, 132
   give and take in, 70
   personnel relations and, 10

vacation
   enjoyment of, 141–144
   fear of, 141
   need for, 53
   planning of, 143–144
value judgments
   proper employment of, 204
   risk management and, 165
Vroom, Victor, 101

Wall Street Journal, 49
way of life, changes in, 76–78
weight control, health and, 85, 151
Who's Who, 37
wife
   family relationships and, 146–147
   in planning timetable, 187
   preparation of in impending change, 13